Conduit 4 seen in Princess Street depot-approach during the Centenary Year 1985

PROLOGUE OF THE CONDUIT TRAMWAY INAUGURATION

Tuesday 29th September 1885 proved to be a fete day for Blackpool, with the official opening of the new tramway and the launching of a new lifeboat. The local newspaper, while admitting that electric traction had already been tried elsewhere, dismissed these early trials: "Other towns have given the lead in adopting electricity as a motive power for a tramway, but use in the case of Brighton Volks Railway is little more than a toy and Giants Causeway Tramway in Northern Ireland is of a type entirely different. Undoubtedly Holroyd Smith's conduit system has introduced the electric tramway car to the streets of Britain, and made urban mass-transportation for the first time".

"Handsome in design and elegant in every detail of its construction, the car was brought immediately opposite the lifeboat launching ground, here number 5 came and away it went without assistance, showing the magic of adapted human knowledge. The crowd near the tramway and on the North Pier was simply astounding. Mr. Holroyd Smith had the honour to demonstrate the use of electricity as a motive power for tramway propulsion. He presented Ald. Harwood, the Mayor of Manchester and opener of the line, with an ebony and brass handle, on which was inscribed: "His Worship inaugurating the Blackpool Electric Tramway, September 29th 1885". Incidentally a century later in 1985, the original ebony and brass handle was produced by the Harwood family and used to drive conduit-car 4 at the head of the twenty-tram Centenary procession again on 29th September.

However, the success of the two mile line along the Promenade was somewhat thwarted by its exposure to wind and tide from the Irish Sea. So strong were the periodic storms, that the waves washed over the tram rails and filled the conduit grooved rail with water and sand, thus earthing the current. The generator was situated behind the depot in Blundell Street and could produce a maximum power of 300 volts, but there was a loss of power to 230 volts at Foxhall , 185 volts at Cocker Street northern end, and 168 volts at Victoria Pier southern end. On occasions horses pulled the trams, and when the Corporation took over from the Electric Railway Company in 1892, there was a desire to replace the conduit system with overhead line. This was encouraged by the opening of the Blackpool & Fleetwood Tramroad in 1898, and thus their tramway was re-equipped in 1899.

Conduit-car 4 on the Promenade having just passed Robert's Oyster Bar, with the driver holding a control-handle projecting through the stairway, and the hand-brake with his other hand. (Roy Hubble collection)

JOHN LANCASTER - Tramway Manager 1885 - 1910

Blackpool Electric Tramway Company appointed John Lancaster as Traffic Manager before the tramway opened, and was paid £1-15s a week. When the Company lease expired in 1892, he was retained and became the first Electric Tramway Manager. He presided over the transformation from the conduit system to the overhead line in 1899, and the extension of the system to Gynn Square, and routes to Marton, Layton and South Shore via Lytham Road. While the creator of the conduit system was Holroyd Smith, Cornelius Quin took care of the electrical side of the operation and John Lancaster managed the day-to-day running of the tramway. He was concerned about the condition of labour for men, reducing their hours, and improving of pay and conditions of uniform. About his men Lancaster is quoted as saying: "A tramway servant is now regarded as a responsible public servant and not, as formerly a drudge". He maintained a kindly interest in welfare matters, instituting an annual reunion for former employees, together with an annual tea-party for their children, over which he presided.

Tramroad crossbench car with its crew and inspector at the Talbot Road Station terminus in 1898. (A.D. Packer Collection)

During John Lancaster's period, one of the most notable affairs was the arrival of George Shrewsbury at the Tramway Committee in February 1897. He brought a set of plans and a model of a tram with double-staircases at each end fitted with fixed boarding steps. Blackpool bought the patent rights for this new tram for £12, and the first two were built by George F. Milnes at Birkenhead. Nos. 15 & 16 were delivered in July 1898 and went into service during August Bank Holiday. The Electrical Review Magazine stated that while these cars were operating on the conduit system, there was a feeling that this was a major problem. Lancaster and Quin agreed in having a deep and sustained hatred of the conduit system. By this time there had been twelve years of struggling in maintaining a tram service along the Promenade, both by the unreliable trams and the filling of conduit with sand. Certainly the final piece of conduit track was opened on August 7th 1897 in Station Road, linking the Lytham Road line with the Promenade at Victoria (South) Pier. Following this, the Council were recommended that the whole system by 1898 should be converted to overhead wires. Quin indicated that the conversion of the system would cost no more than £10,000, however permission was refused by the Board of Trade, stating that the overhead wire system could be susceptible to breaking in the wind. Fortunately the Board of Trade relented, and in June 1898 agreed to the proposal for rewiring the Blackpool tramway. The right decision was confirmed on July 1st 1898 by the opening of the Blackpool & Fleetwood Tramroad with an inaugural run by crossbench car 4 from Talbot Road Station to Fleetwood at 3-10 p.m.. The invited Municipal party included Lancaster and Quin, which confirmed the decision about their system would be better. The ride was over the cliffs at some speed towards Bispham and Cleveleys, and then through the farming fields towards Fleetwood. As the tram arrived at Ash Street they were greeted by the cheering crowd of school children. No.4 was parked near London Street, and was admired by a local crowd, while the party went for lunch in the Mount Hotel. Ald. Cocker commented that "The feeling was grand" about the new journey, and proposed a toast to the Company's success.

Having extended the tramway to Gynn Square in 1900, a Dreadnought is seen here passing the Imperial Hotel of 1867. Notice the trolley angle-working and the bracket-arms with wrought-iron. (Author's Collection)

In Blackpool after the Season, work started on the new overhead. The existing bracket-arms were fitted through the poles, so that they could be repositioned on the other side when the Promenade was widened in 1905. The overhead wires were off-centre, so that the trolley-poles on the trams were twenty feet long, thus reaching the overhead at an angle. The Lytham Road scheme for centre poles was rejected, and thus side poles and span-wires were chosen. On June 7th 1899 a tram went out with a trolley on the overhead wires, while still drawing its power from the conduit. At midnight the overhead was live, and cars 9 and 12 gave a successful demonstration. On June 21st approval was given to the Promenade line to Cocker Street. While the overhead went live, the conduit system stayed active until June 23rd when it was used finally, as an end to the 1885 experiment.

NEW DEVELOPMENTS WITH DREADNOUGHT TRAMS

Since the Claremont Park Estate north of Cocker Street had been taken over by the Borough, a three-tiered promenade was constructed between 1896 and 1899. Thus it was possible to extend the tramway to Gynn Square, and therefore meet the Blackpool & Fleetwood Tramroad to facilitate journeys northwards. There had been consideration of putting the new tramway on to the Middle Walk, but this was rejected by the vote of ratepayers, and therefore construction began on the carriageway after the 1899 season. Conduit track from Church Street to Cocker Street was lifted and replaced by double-track to link the new line to Gynn Square. The first Dreadnought 17 was delivered in mid-January 1900, having been built by Midland Carriage & Wagon Company. 17 -26 were four feet longer than 15 & 16, which were thus extended by two fitters who were also assembling the new trams. John Lancaster declared about the Dreadnoughts: "It was my idea of the perfect car for Blackpool". About the first arrival of 17 he said: "She is the most handsome car in England and I am proud of her". 17 made its first trial-run on the evening of February 19th, and went into service soon after. By the middle of March, the Promenade winter service was operated by Dreadnoughts, while the ex-conduit cars operated on Lytham Road. On May 24th Dreadnought 24 travelled over the new three-quarter mile extension to Gynn Square with two inspectors walking in front of it, though both rode on its return journey to South Shore. Col. Yorke asked why the front steps of 24 were fixed in position, and John Lancaster replied that: "They were just right for Blackpool traffic". At the beginning of operation, John Lancaster staffed the 92 seat Dreadnoughts by two conductors, and introduced "passenger-flow" at each stop, with passengers getting on at the back and off at the front. However Transport Union members complained that the public were coming down the front stairs and also through the saloon doorway, thus pushing past the driver and hindering him from braking. The Board of Trade agreed with this, and prevented this procedure for safety, but it was still possible when the trams were stopped at the terminus. In 1900 Blundell Street depot was enlarged to accommodate the new trams, having a higher roof, being wider and extended its length to Rigby Road. The capacity of fleet was doubled to forty, and thus trams and earning profits had increased.

MARTON & LAYTON ROUTES

The expansion of the tramway system continued with the opening of the Marton route from Talbot Square to Central Station on May 23rd 1901. While there were 3.5 miles of double-track and half a mile of single-track in Church Street and on the inner part of Central Drive. Incidentally there was only a short walking distance between the two termini. The line served the rural communities to the east of the town, and was subject to heavy losses until the development of housing and Stanley Park in the Twenties. Unfortunately the opening of the route was dogged by problems, arising from the wider groove of the rail, which was deemed to be dangerous to cyclists. Therefore on the opening day, with inspection by the Board of Trade, car 32 was stopped in Church Street by two cycles and a banner between them showing: SUICIDE MADE EASY - RIDE ON THESE TRAM LINES.

Falbot Square and Entrance to North Pier, Blackpool.

A view from Yates's Wine Lodge in 1902, showing a Marton car on the left-hand side of the shelter, and Layton track on the right side.

North Promenades, Blackpool

North Promenade with the new track to Gynn Square in 1900, and a Dreadnought going south.

Gynn Inn, Blackpool.

A famous scene of Promenade trams meeting the Tramroad cars at the Gynn Inn, newly-arrived in 1900. The Cabin can be seen on the left-hand side of the track, at the top of the hill. (Author's Collection)

(Above) Inside Blundell Street depot as extended in 1900, with the staff posing in front of Marton Box-car and Dreadnought 16. (Below) The South Shore terminus just beyond Victoria Pier, showing four Dreadnoughts loading simultaneously, with passengers boarding large steps and double stairs. (Studio D)

Dreadnought 61 fully-loaded and one of twenty-five trams decorated for the 1902 Coronation of King Edward VII, here seen in North shore en-route for The Gynn. (Daphne Luff)

The open-top new trams 27-41 with four-wheel trucks, had problems by breaking their axles in the first two weeks, caused by the track-fan of Marton depot, which had to be relaid. In the following year a one-mile route from Talbot Square to Layton was opened on June 19th 1902, and it was never attractive because it terminated at the Cemetery and passed the railway goods yard, Abbatoir, Sanatorium and Thwaites brewery en-route. A two-class system was introduced, with penny tickets for riding on the open top-deck and 2d for riding in the saloon of the small ex-conduit cars. This was soon discontinued for lack of patronage. However twelve new Hurst Nelson open-top bogie cars 42 - 53 built at Motherwell were introduced on Lytham Road route and Dreadnoughts 54-61 were bought for the Promenade. After these, there were no new trams for nine years.

In June 1902 twenty-five trams were decorated for the Coronation of King Edward VII & Queen Alexandra, with free riding for school children in the Borough, which they used to full advantage. However, because of the illness of the King, the Coronation was postponed until 9th August. Happily the school children were once again given free-riding and resumed their advantage. In this year the Borough Electrical Engineer Cornelius Quin left Blackpool and was replaced by Charles Furness. At this time John Lancaster wanted the Tramway and Electrical Departments separated, but he did not succeed. Eventually Charles Furness - his successor as Tramway Manager in 1911 - felt the same way and succeeded in 1932 when Walter Luff became Transport General Manager. On May 30th in the same year work began in widening the Promenade between South Shore and Alexandra Road, to the width of 100 feet, including separate reservation for the tramway, between the road and pedestrian precinct. The traction poles remained in the same position, with bracket-arms being on the seaside and decorated with scrollwork. They had already been surmounted by street lights. This new promenade layout facilitated the progress of the trams, and passengers safely boarded away from the road traffic. Work continued with the wide promenade towards Central Pier in 1904, leaving Central Promenade to be completed by April 20th 1905.

A handsome postcard view of Central Promenade showing the extended layout in 1905, with the reserved track for the trams. Here is seen one of the Lancaster trams 11-14 heading north.
(Below)
An attractive view of former-conduit trams at North Pier in 1899, seen from Theatre Royal with the Talbot Square fountain in the foreground. It can be seen that they now have long trolley-poles and are both Lancaster cars 3 - 6 in different colours according to the artist. (Both Author's Collection)

20th ANNIVERSARY OF THE TRAMWAY

In 1903 there was extension of the line from South Pier to the entrance of the new fairground, where a four-track layout was provided for trams to be loading and unloading side-by-side. To give access, a short single-track was provided between this and the approaching double-track. Undoubtedly this would become the busiest terminus on the system, since W.G. Bean had created a American-style Amusement Park, which was enhanced in 1904 by Sir Hiram Maxim's flying machine. It is still going today at the Pleasure Beach, after which the Amusement Park was named in 1906. In the following year the Board of Trade questioned Blackpool: "Why does Mr.Lancaster not have sand-boxes and pipes attached to every car?" and "All trams should have gate and tray lifeguards". By the time of the 20th Anniversary of the tramway in 1905, there were eight illuminated trams and 1885 car 3 was beautifully decorated for the occasion. Its upper deck panels bore PROGRESS 1885 - 1905 in lights, while at each end a sign read: FIRST ELECTRIC STREET TRAMCAR IN THE KINGDOM - STILL RUNNING. Undoubtedly the coincidence of this and the "Auspicious Opening of the New Promenade" on 25th July 1905, made Blackpool's greatest day. On that day Blackpool celebrated the completion of one of the greatest works undertaken: the reclamation of 22 acres of land from the sea, and the construction of a line of sea-defences. On the magnificent Promenade and terraces, the Corporation had spent half-a-million pounds and it created work for hundreds of men. Thousands of people flocked to the new Promenade on that day, together with 5,000 Primary School children, who watched the procession. The children were given the newly-prepared commemorative handkerchiefs; on these were shown the new Central Promenade scene, complete with the Tower, sea-wall and tramway with Dreadnought trams, surmounted by the Borough coat-of-arms. Undoubtedly this year marked the end of major development of Blackpool Tramway for some time. There were 61 trams in the fleet, but profits were affected by the recession in the cotton industry. Undoubtedly John Lancaster had successfully managed the new tramway system, and he completed 25 years with his death in 1910. The local press said: "Blackpool has lost one of its oldest and most devoted public officials".

Manager John Lancaster standing in front of No.3 in Blundell Street depot, especially decorated for the 25th Anniversary of the tramway in 1905: "FIRST ELECTRIC TRAMWAY IN THE KINGDOM - STILL RUNNING" (Author's Collection)

A delightful scene in Whitegate Drive with Toastrack 69 and Motherwell 40 posed for the photograph. (Right) Charles Furness, Electrical Engineer 1902-1936, & Tramway Engineer 1910-1932.

PROLOGUE OF CHARLES FURNESS 1910 - 1932

Charles Furness was unique in the history of Blackpool Tramways in occupying two major posts: Borough Electrical Engineer 1902 - 1936 and Tramways Manager 1910 - 1932. It was not surprising that upon his retirement in January 1936, he was quoted in saying: "A man cannot serve two masters, therefore I am a man without a hobby!" After taking over the Tramways Department following the sudden death of John Lancaster, Charles Furness became responsible for several innovations. Firstly he introduced new cars, including de-Luxe cars 62 - 68, new Pullman cars 167 - 176 fitted with pantographs for the Fleetwood route and the famous Toastracks which inaugurated the Circular Tour. Of course he also supervised the integration of the Borough Tramway with the Blackpool & Fleetwood Tramroad Company in 1920. Thirdly he was responsible for the Illuminations which first started in 1912 and was revived in 1925 after the failure of the Carnival.

With these achievements to his credit, one would have thought he would have the support of the Council, but unfortunately they seemed to disagree with some of his proposals. However Furness was strong and forceful by nature and wielded power in his two Departments, although he was always just and fair with his employees. He resisted the demands of the Council for change by introduction of bus routes in place of trams, and he campaigned for the retention of the tramway routes. While bus services were introduced in the Twenties, they never conflicted with the tramway services. When the Council did not sanction a fleet of new trams, Charles Furness instituted a programme of tram building in the new workshops, under the guise of rebuilding older trams.

In 1929 the name of the Tramways Department was changed to Blackpool Corporation Transport, in recognition of its wider operation by buses. In 1932 the growth of both Charles Furness' responsibilities was such that a new Transport Manager - Walter Luff - was appointed from 1933, and Charles Furness continued as Electrical Engineer until his retirement in 1936. On this occasion his achievements were measured by the £160,000 which his two Departments had contributed to rate-relief during his tenure. The Gazette said: "No man is more deserving of the ratepayers' thanks than Mr. Furness, whose enthusiasm and enterprise has made both his Departments a wonderful source of revenue for the town. Of course, he must also be the man who saved Blackpool trams!"

EVENTS UNDER CHARLES FURNESS

Having been the Borough Engineer from 1902, Charles Furness was appointed as the second Manager of Blackpool Tramways, following the sudden death of John Lancaster in March 1910. He was undoubtedly a specialist in the electrical industry, and thus he was responsible for several innovations, including the Illuminations and the Circular Tour, which began on August Bank Holiday 1911. In order to operate the new service, twenty four toastracks 69 - 92 were built by the United Electric Car Company, and provided between 1911 and 1914. This innovation was a reaction to the increasingly popular excursions by char-a-bancs. Charles Furness saw that these open electric trams would be ideal to attract patronage by the visitors, and certainly became profitable notably between the two World Wars. The enlarged Marton depot became ideal as the location for the 24 toastracks, using four tracks on the east side of the depot. From here the toastracks travelled round to Talbot Square, where the terminus siding was linked with the Promenade track enabling large queues to form, while the Marton service cars reversed on the single-track outside Yates's Wine Lodge. At a fare of 6d, the Tour comprised a journey along the Promenade to South Pier, where it crossed to Station Road, turned into Lytham Road at South Station, and right into Waterloo Road at Royal Oak. It certainly provided the Circular sensation at Oxford Square when the trams turned left into Whitegate Drive and again at Devonshire Square where they turned left into Talbot Road. It became a ritual for each Toastrack to stop outside the Oxford Hotel where a photographer captured the passengers on each tour.

Undoubtedly the new Circular Tour proved popular from 1911, as seen here with the crowd boarding 70 in Talbot Square. Motherwell 48 is seen in front of the Town Hall on the Marton route. (Studio D)

His assistant always held a code-number in front of the group, by which the passengers could identify their photograph afterwards in Talbot Square and buy it. This was ceased in 1927, owing to busy traffic and increased frequency of the tram service. Also the Corporation originally commissioned a postcard of a loaded toastrack in Whitegate Drive, albeit going in the opposite direction into the sun. The success of the Circular Tour was confirmed by the addition of six more Toastracks in 1927, built by Blackpoool Transport in the workshops, with Dick Kerr equipment. The extension of South Promenade in 1926 resulted in Circular Tour to Squires Gate in 1932, and the fare rose to 9d. This was the final year of Charles Furness as General Manager.

The first illuminated car De-Luxe 68 being fitted with its light bulbs each year, from 1912 until finally replaced by the Bandwagon in 1937. Standards 158 & 159 resembled 68 from 1959! (Author's Collection)

Two interesting scenes in Blundell Street depot: (left) during World War 1 women producing shell-cases (right) new sides are being assembled for a Motherwell car, and the bogies are seen in the foreground with the top-cover behind it. This took place before the new Works were assembled in 1920. (Author's Collection)

In 1912 Charles Furness introduced new De-Luxe car 68 as the first illuminated car for the first illuminations to celebrate the opening of Princess Parade in front of Metropole Hotel by Princess Louise. De-Luxe 68 was described by the Blackpool Times as "the cynosure of all eyes". The seven De-Luxe cars had been built by U.E.C. at Preston, and with rattan seats were luxurious compared with the rest of the fleet. The first three 62 - 64 were smaller with four-wheel trucks and seated 64 passengers, while the other four 65 - 68 seated 78 passengers. Being unvestibuled, the crew called them "shower-baths", while the saloons had full-drop glass windows for the passengers. These cars provided examples for the Standards, which were to be made by the Transport Department in the Twenties. Royal visits - notably that of King George V & Queen Mary on 8th July 1913 - provided open-top trams lined-up along the Promenade as grandstands for the public viewing, costing 1/- each. It was notable that these trams earned more than collecting normal tram fares along the Promenade. The First World War undoubtedly intervened between future tramway development, however Charles Furness' great financial success was the manufacture of shell-cases in Blundell Street depot, where 200,000 were produced and largely by female labour. This produced a profit of circa £24,000 by the Borough, which was subsequently used for the erection the Cenotaph War-memorial on Princess Parade. Also during the First World War, Blackpool accommodated troops under training, and convalescent soldiers were accommodated at Squires Gate, known as "The Camp", and were taken for tours of Blackpool by toastracks. Finally, Blackpool Tramways produced a replica tank named Albert, based on one of the former conduit cars. It travelled round the town with wounded soldiers selling raffle tickets in aid of the war-funds. Thus a key part was played by Charles Furness, and in post-war years new developments took place.

Tramroad Company "Yank"31 at the Dickson Road terminus, has reversed for Fleetwood. Notice the large oil lamp mounted on the dash-panel and a spot-light mounted on the roof, together with the running-board for entering the crossbench seats. A Box-car is waiting for departure further away. (Lens of Sutton)

ACQUISITION OF THE BLACKPOOL & FLEETWOOD TRAMROAD COMPANY

The days of the Tramroad Company were numbered once Blackpool Corporation extended its boundary to Cleveleys, following the take-over of Bispham-with-Norbreck on 1st April 1917. Already the Tramroad track was owned within the Borough just beyond Gynn Square, and therefore Blackpool sought how they could bring the whole Tramroad within their grasp, since the Company had always been a profitable operator. The Tramroad Directors passed a resolution to be offered to the Lancashire & Yorkshire Railway Company for £225,000. However secret negotiations were taking place between Manager John Cameron and Ald. Lindsay Parkinson Mayor of Blackpool. In fact he made a higher bid of £235,000 and the Borough purchased the Tramroad Company from 1st January 1918. Giving the Company operating rights for two years, Blackpool took possession on 1st January 1920, and John Cameron finally collected his mail at Bispham depot and returned to his home of "Pooldhooie", which is there today as the Conservative Club. Bispham depot was still run by his sons, Angus and Tommy Cameron, who were in charge of the depot and power station. However there were busy scenes at Gynn Square, where gangs of workmen were making a sharp curve between the promenade terminus and the Tramroad line. By 1924 a better junction was made when the promenade track was re-aligned on to reservation up to the Cabin. A junction was also made at Talbot Road Station, between the Dickson Road terminus and the Layton route. Some signs of the Tramroad Company lasted for some time, for Blackpool had acquired a well-maintained system and a staff who were proud of their service and wore company uniforms until worn-out and replaced.

Charles Furness proposed increasing the service from 15-minutes to 10-minute headway. The new time-table appeared on April 1st 1920, when FLEETWOOD was added to the list of services for the first time. The first car from Talbot Road terminus in the morning was at 6-45 a.m., and the last car was at 10-45 p.m.. To operate this service Blackpool had only fifteen saloon cars, but twenty-six crossbench cars making an unbalanced fleet, and they were renumbered 101 - 141. Mr. Furness thus proposed to make a futher six saloons from the "Yank California" cars of 1900, and it was the first rebuilding job to be undertaken in the new Rigby Road workshops, housed in the former aircraft hangars. They were subsequent known by the staff as "Glasshouses". The new numbers 101 -115 for saloons, Yanks 116 - 122 and Crossbench-cars 123 - 141, were the only indication of changes, since the Company name and the livery of chocolate-and-cream were still carried by the cars. The first repaint into the red-and-white livery was carried out in March 1920, described by the local press as "Particularly smart in appearance and all advertisements have been removed from the outside of the car. The interior and exterior lighting have been approved, and the interior received some artistic treatment." It must have been quite a sight to see the cars still in the Company livery travelling down the Promenade for the first time. As far as staff at Bispham depot were concerned, nothing had changed! Many of the staff continued as before, and for years until its closure on 27th October 1963, Bispham depot was known as "the other firm". It is interesting to recall that the driver of the last tram from North Station was Tom Leeming, the last of the Tramroad Company drivers.

In 1920 the Corporation had acquired 41 trams from the Tramroad Company and it already had 88 cars of its own, and it had added eight miles of the Fleetwood route to its own 9.75 mile of its own system. The town system had been compact with a network of overlapping services, but now it was possible to extend services northwards beyond Gynn Square. However, Charles Furness reported that three-quarters of the system needed relaying, and planned that it would extend over three years until completed before the 1923 season. The cost of this work, which would include the relaying of the Marton route at £110,867 and doubling of the Dickson Road track to Gynn Square, was £254,343. Adding to this was the cost of new works, including laying sidings at Thornton Gate for the mineral traffic, diverting the track at Rossall and extending the terminus to Fleetwood Ferry. Clearly there was quite a challenge of progress, and Charles Furness was determined that it ensured the future of the tramway.

"Glasshouse"117 after being rebuilt as a saloon car. Notice it retains its opening quarter-lights, while it has new quarter-lights on the saloon windows complete with scrolled patterns. Seen here at Gynn Square it is bound for Pleasure Beach. (Author's Collection)

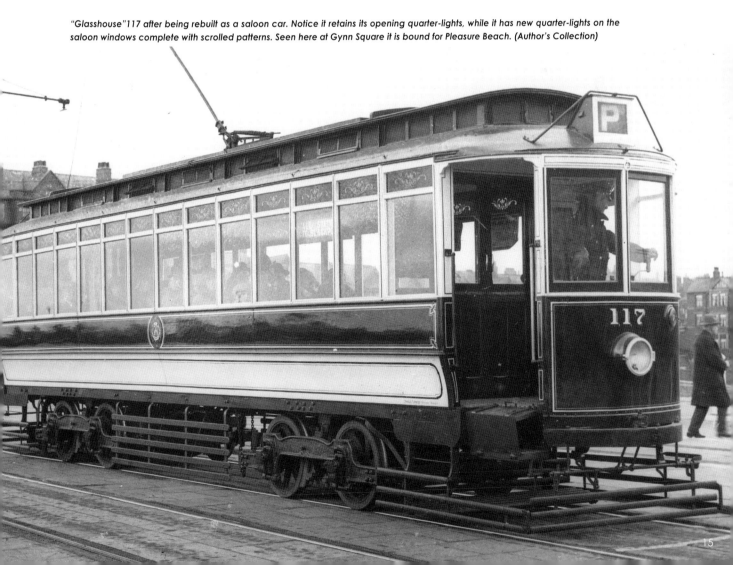

NEW DEVELOPMENTS INAUGURATED MUNICIPAL BUSES

A significant event of note was an inspection of a 30 seat Tilling Stevens petrol-electric bus on 6th March 1920. Under the terms of the 1919 Act, the Corporation was obliged to provide a tram or bus service between Cleveleys Square and Thornton Station. Since it would run through the countryside a bus service was the only alternative, and the Corporation started operation in July 1921 with two buses, which were garaged at Thornton Gate. Charles Furness was convinced that these buses would never pay, since they stood at Thornton Station to meet trains, and at Cleveleys waiting for customers. However in 1921, within the Borough it was suggested that buses should operate between Palatine Road and Oxford Square during the reconstruction of the Marton tram track. Clearly this suggestion was seen as the future development of bus service in Blackpool. Certainly Mr. Furness was keen to improve delays on the tramway services, as seen in the doubling of the Layton route between Devonshire Road hospital and Princess laundry passing-loop in 1920. It was also important to double the track in Church Street between Winter Gardens and the Hippodrome, at the expense of St. John's churchyard. In November 1921 negotiations were in progress with the Fleetwood Estates Company for an exchange of land at Rossall, so that the sharp curve there could be eliminated and Broadway constructed. When there had been a Miners' strike in April 1921, all tram services within the Borough had to be suspended on Sundays, and charabanc proprietors were allowed to carry passengers along the tram routes. This stimulated the idea of bus versatility and there was further agitation against the tramway in 1922, although Charles Furness treated the suggestions with scant ceremony. However, four petro-electric motor buses inaugurated the first bus service within the Borough between Adelaide Place and Caunce Street in December 1922, serving an area between the Marton and Layton tram routes.

First Standard 33 seen on the traverser outside the Car Body Shop of the new Works. Notice it has maximum-traction bogies from a Motherwell car, and it has replaced Marton Box-car 33. (Author's Collection)

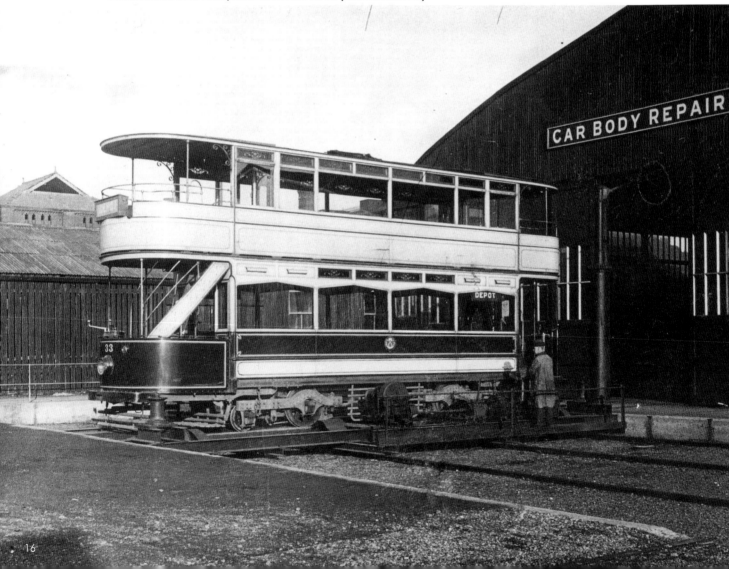

In 1921 a busy scene in Abingdon Street as a new double-track is constructed here for the Marton route. Notice the trench round the track to receive tar, and the boilers providing it. (W.R. Buckley)

Once the 1922 season was over, track relaying started on Dickson Road and on Central Drive, with a consequent interruption to service. The track in Dickson Road was being doubled during relaying, since the single-track sections had resulted in delays to services. A single-line circular service was in operation, with the inward cars to North Station turned into Talbot Road, and carried Fleetwood passengers back along the Promenade. The Central Drive renewal also resulted in changes, since Lytham St Annes cars were diverted to operate along Lytham Road and the Promenade to a terminus at Talbot Square. This marked the first appearance of the "Blue-cars" on Blackpool Promenade, since it had been the policy to exclude them from the busiest route. The only service maintained in Central Drive was a single-line "special" between Central Station and South Shore Station in Lytham Road. The Marton service was diverted, and instead of turning right into Central Drive continued to Royal Oak where it turned right into Lytham Road, and proceeded to Talbot Square. Here the cars reversed and returned the same way, thus making it a circular route. There was criticism at the time that the Lytham Road service cars reversed at Highfield Road, leaving the "Blue-cars" carrying passengers to Squires Gate. A local resident commented; "Now we are packed like sardines into small St. Annes cars". Soon the Corporation cars were restored to Squires Gate, and "Blue-cars" permanently operated along the Promenade.

In February 1923, the ordering of three petrol-electric buses by the Transport Committee, the bodies for which would be constructed at Rigby Road works, resulted in criticism on the Council. Mr Furness being an electrician "naturally leaned towards an electrical form of propulsion". Clearly a time of controversy had arrived, and the Mayor said that it took longer to train on a bus with gears than the ten days taken to train a tram or a petro-electric bus driver. However it was clear that the bus would become a permanent part of the Blackpool scene.

NEW DEVELOPMENTS OF THE TRAMWAY SYSTEM

More constructive developments were taking place elsewhere on the system. With the increase of motor traffic in the Twenties, the narrow North Promenade, with the street tramway dominating the road was quite a problem. It was therefore proposed to move the tramway to a paved reservation west of the road, and the Promenade had to be widened by constructing colonnades over the slope down to Middle Walk. This was an ambitious scheme and took several years to complete between Cocker Street and Gynn Square. Further improvements towards the end of 1923 included the conversion of the former light-railway from Gynn Square to the Cabin to a paved reservation, and this would enable double-deck cars to operate there. The old Gynn Inn had closed in May 1921 and was demolished in August, making more room for traffic in the Square. Therefore the tramway reservation was constructed between the sunken gardens and the carriageway, with a loop line round the shelter. This would create a turning facility for the Lytham St. Annes trams there. Meanwhile at Cleveleys Victoria Square there was a need to demolish the traditional tram station, which obstructed the Brighton Avenue and Victoria Road junction. In September 1924 work began in re-aligning the track in the Square, which had become a busy crossroads. In the same month a new terminus was authorised at Fleetwood, which would take the trams beyond North Albert Street terminus on a new single-line loop to the Ferry where there would be a siding, and return along Pharos Street passing the lighthouse. The pressure of all this work on Blackpool, meant that the period during which new tramway could be constructed under the 1919 Act had expired by 1924. Further extensions of existing routes - those at Layton and South Shore – would have needed the approval of a Parliamentary Act. At Layton it was proposed to extend the route from the Cemetery to Bispham (now Layton) Station, but there was a lot of opposition to the Charles Furness proposal. The South Shore scheme would take the tramway beyond the Pleasure Beach to link up with the Lytham St. Annes track in Clifton Drive. The Council expressed reservations about this, since there would be little passenger potential until more development of hotels had taken place. However New South Promenade was opened on 2nd October 1926 by Lord Derby, who also opened the new Stanley Park. It is true that an agreement with the Pleasure Beach Company insisted that all passing trams showed on the indicators SOUTH PROMENADE via PLEASURE BEACH. Certainly hotel crescents, gardens and a boating pool at Harrowside justified extending the tramway.

A charming scene of Standard 146 at Layton terminus, with the Cemetery behind the fenced-wall.

A scene of the new Pleasure Beach terminus in the Twenties, the track-layout facilitating a through track for South Promenade in 1926. While many Dreadnoughts can be seen, there is a former Tramroad Box-car as a newcomer here. You will be interested to identify Pleasure Beach rides, including the original Hiram Maxim Flying Machine. (Gazette)

By July 1925 there were signs of improvements in the operation of Blackpool Tramways, in ten weeks receipts were £10,000 more than the previous year. In April plans for a new track layout at the Pleasure Beach were drawn-up to replace the four-track stub of 1910. This would provide through-running to South Promenade, as well as providing terminal sidings. In Fleetwood, Lt. Col. Mount of the Ministry of Transport inspected the new Ferry loop-line and the Rossall shortened-line on 23rd July. Thus trams were given a more prominent terminus at Fleetwood, and passengers could board the Knott End ferry and easily walk to the Jubilee Quay for boats to the Isle of Man, Barrow or Belfast. At Rossall School the tram stop had moved further away, leaving the passengers' brick shelter behind. Later in that year it was dismantled and rebuilt at the corner of Rossall Lane and Broadway, where it is today. During the winter, it was proposed to relay the line between Cabin and Bispham, to enable double-deck trams to use it by Easter 1926.

ILLUMINATIONS RESTORED WITH GONDOLA & LIFEBOAT

A significant achievement happened in 1925 when the Illuminations, which ceased in 1914 because of World War 1, was revived by popular demand following the chaos of the Carnival in 1924. When the illuminations was inaugurated in 1912, the newest De-Luxe car was decorated by 3,000 bulbs, and the effect was stunning when it toured the suburbs and Lytham St.Annes. In 1925 there was need for a new illuminated tram, and so the Gondola was created from the underframe and 4-wheel truck of Marton Box 28. In the Body Shop where replacing Standard 28 was subsequently created in 1927, the Gondola was made most elegant, with high curved prow, graceful pagoda-style roof and hull decorated with gold-leaf scrollwork. Undoubtedly the nautical effect was enhanced by painted marine canvas covering the 4-wheel truck. Twenty passengers could board by a ladder over the side, and be seated on rattan-cane seats. However, in the first season the driver and guard were dressed as Venetian gondoliers, much to the amusement of other tram crews. While the Gondola did not carry paying passengers, its seats were occupied by guests or a small orchestra playing "The Gondoliers". The 1925 Illuminations attracted an additional million passengers to the Promenade trams, bringing an extra revenue of £7,360. Thus in 1926 a third illuminated car was created as a Lifeboat built from Marton Box 40, by Tramway Engineer Freddie Field in commemoration of the Golden Jubilee of Blackpool Borough. Thus it was named "Jubilee", shown on the Borough coat of arms, and its reversible sails comprised of strings in white lights. Its dark hull was illuminated by loops of lights simulating the safety-ropes, while waves of green lights represented the sea below. The 1926 Illuminations had to be terminated prematurely because of the Miners' Strike, however they were restored for one night on October 2nd for the opening of New South Promenade. Since Stanley Park was also opened on the same day by Lord Derby, it gave the Marton route more customers to sample the 26-acre boating lake, bowling-greens gardens and cricket ground.

Womens Liberal Federation in 1926, making a busy tramway scene at North Pier, with ladies wearing cloche hats and coats. Officials of Blackpool Transport are in the foreground, including Inspector Jack Parkinson and the General Manager. (Studio D)

FINAL INTEGRATION OF THE SYSTEMS

Once the North Promenade was competed in 1926, it became possible to operate the Lytham St.Annes cars to Gynn Square, where they reversed and used a siding. Until this time no through-car service had operated along the Promenade to Fleetwood, and thus Talbot Road Station had remained the only such terminus. Once the relaying of the track to Bispham was complete, the Promenade service was extended northwards on 25th June 1926, and so the double-deckers were seen here for the first time. In many ways the 1926 Season represented the logical conclusion of the 1920 Tramroad take-over. The time-table included greatly increased headways on all routes, as seen on the list:-

1926 SEASON SERVICES

PROMENADE	South Shore & Uncle Tom's Cabin	8 minutes
SQUIRES GATE	Talbot Square & Squires Gate	6 minutes (new)
	North Shore & Squires Gate	12 minutes
MARTON	Talbot Square & Central Station	8 minutes
	Central Station & Royal Oak	8 minutes
	Talbot Square & Royal Oak	8 minutes
	Talbot Square & Marton	4 minutes (new)
LAYTON	Talbot Square & Layton	6 minutes
FLEETWOOD	Talbot Road Station & Fleetwood	12 minutes

One of the six newly-built Toastracks. 161-166 outside Marton Depot 1927.
(Below) Electric locomotive with wagons at Thornton Gate siding from 1927-1949. (F.Wohrman)

(Opposite)
Pantograph car 173 heads for Fleetwood at Gynn Square, its tower looking tall.
(Right) Toastrack 90 as the first Circular Tour extension on South Promenade 1932.
(Below) Scene in Cleveleys Square with Box car 111 and Pantograph 176 with newly-laid track and the shelter to be demolished.
(Author's Collection)

NEW DEVELOPMENTS ON THE TRAMWAY

In 1927 the final aspect of the Tramroad company take-over took place, with the opening of Thornton Gate sidings, and the sight of railway wagons being pulled by an electric-loco. This was built by Dick Kerr Co. of Preston, painted in red with lining and white lettering: BLACKPOOL CORPORATION ENGINEERING DEPT.. Thus began the regular sight of railway wagons loaded with coal, from the railway at the rear of Copse Road depot to the coal merchants at Thornton Gate siding. Although this lasted only 22 years until 30th April 1949, the author and those who lived along the tramway can remember the clanking of buffers. Certainly its slow speed delayed the service cars which slowly followed the train on a busy Market day. Each train had a flag–carrying guard, who stopped the road-traffic at Broadwater and Rossall Road-crossings. Upon the return of the empty wagons in the afternoon, they were pushed by the loco with the guard in the front one, signalling the driver with the red and green flags. In those days the road-crossings had sleeper-track and not the street track that it does today. In 1949 the coal merchants decided to collect coal from railway sidings at Thornton Station, which was quicker than on the tramway. The electric loco was then used to tow the rail-carrier to track-work on the tramway, but today at the National Tramway Museum it moves trams to and from the depot, without the railway buffers.

In 1928, the arrival of modern trams for the Fleetwood route gave great impetus to the inter-urban operation. Built by Dick Kerr Co. of Preston, 167 – 176 were notable by being fitted with pantographs, but were originally called Pullman-cars. Undoubtedly they were handsome in appearance, had wide platforms for carrying luggage, a saloon with six large windows and 44 upholstered seats, together with two leather seats on each platform. They only operated the North Station & Fleetwood route, and were based at Bispham depot for their whole life. At first, they only showed a route-letter for their destination at the front and places en-route on side-indicator boxes.

It is true that the overhead on the Fleetwood route was lightly-suspended to facilitate the pantographs. To ensure their smooth operation, the contact-plates had to be greased each day, and it is known that grease was gathered by trolley wheels of other trams, and taken as far as Lytham. When 167 was delivered to Rigby Road at the end of July 1928, it was towed to Bispham depot to avoid damage from the fixed bracket-arms along the Promenade. The known Pantograph cars then operated the Fleetwood route throughout the year, and in the Season were augmented by the old-fashioned Box cars. In 1932 a final section of Queens Promenade was built between Norbreck and Anchorsholme, thus providing competition for trams by coaches and buses.

The Charles Furness era was completed in 1932 by what can be described as a vintage year. The popularity of the Circular Tour meant that there were thirty Toastracks, when an additional six were made by the Body Shop. In 1929, the final Standard car 177 was made from all the remaining spare-parts, totalling 36. Together with six new Toastracks, rebuilding six Yanks to Glasshouses, this totalled 48 trams built. Also interesting in 1932 was the extension of the Circular Tour to Squires Gate, thus lengthening the ride and increasing the fare to 9d. Charles Furness made his final report to the Transport Committee, in which he declared a gross profit of £92,045. The fleet of 167 was in stock, including work cars, three illuminated cars and also the bus fleet of 62 vehicles. At the end of 1932, Charles Furness was only Borough Electrical Engineer, leaving a vacancy for a new Transport Manager. Certainly the pattern of tramway-operation had been firmly established in his time, while the eight bus routes continued extending to newly-developing parts of Blackpool. Certainly this provided a tribute to Charles Furness after twenty-two successful years as Tramway Manager.

PROLOGUE OF WALTER LUFF

by Steve Palmer

General Manager Walter Luff undoubtedly had something of a reputation to revolutionise the Blackpool Tramway with his Five Year Plan. From introducing a new fleet of 116 streamlined trams in the Thirties, to the creation of a United Kingdom version of the American PCC cars in post-war years, so his legend has become memorable. In addition to a total of 141 new trams, the new depot, an Art-Deco Transport Office, three turning circles and also 100 Burlingham centre-entrance buses, his name stands out in the history of Blackpool Transport. While I am not old enough to know him personally, it is fortunate that his daughter Daphne Luff has been able to give us a first-hand impression of a famous Transport Manager. In 2009 it was appropriate that Daphne unveiled her father's name on the side of the original Coronation 304. Thus, whenever you see this handsome tram, the name Walter Luff will remind you as to who ordered it and introduced 25 Coronations to the Blackpool & Fleetwood route. However, as a schoolboy I can remember standing in my bedroom window on a Sunday in July 1952 to watch 304 pass on its journey to Fleetwood Ferry. It looked so different to the familiar railcoaches on that route, and it seemed to lay the foundation for a new generation of trams. In retrospect, 58 years later and anticipating the new articulated cars, it seems it might have been a premature start. Of course, history has to be viewed in retrospect!

Walter Luff and "Mac" Marshall walking on North Pier

(Below) Here is seen the famous trio of English Electric cars outside Blundell Street depot in March 1934, demonstrating a new generation of trams. (Author's Collection)

The first railcoach 200 seen in 1933 on the test-track of the English Electric factory in Strand Road, Preston. Notice all the handsome features of the body, including the stainless-steel fenders, windscreens and sliding-roof panels. It is surmounted by the unique tower and the pantograph. (Author's Collection)

WALTER LUFF - BLACKPOOL GENERAL MANAGER 1933 - 1954

by Daphne Luff

Walter Luff was born on 21st June 1887 in North Yorkshire, and he was the seventh child of Constable George Luff and his wife Mary Jane. His father was a member of the North Yorkshire Constabulary for thirty-one years, but none of his four sons were tall enough to join the Police Force. Walter Luff always looked very impressive while sitting behind a desk, but was only average height when standing. He started work at the head office of the Carlton Iron Company at Ferryhill in North Yorkshire on a salary of eight shillings a week, first as an office-boy and then rose to be Secretary to the Manager. Between 1912 and 1924 he worked in various capacities with Yorkshire West Riding Tramway Company, eventually becoming Assistant General Manager. In 1925 he became Commercial Manager of Yorkshire (West Riding) Electric Tramway Company at a salary of £900 per annum. He married Florence Maynard on November 4th in that year. He was appointed General Manager of Blackpool Corporation Transport on 1st January 1933 at a salary of £1,000 per annum.

Upon arrival he was asked to prepare a plan of reorganisation and modernisation of the entire undertaking: trams, buses, depots, office buildings and others. He decided on a "Five Year Plan" of modernisation. Alderman Lumb was Chairman of the Transport Committee and he was a great help and supporter, but he died before the "Five Year Plan" was completed. Ald. Tatham took over and became a staunch supporter of Walter Luff for nearly twenty years, until he died in 1954. Undoubtedly these two Chairmen gave a heaven-sent opportunity for him to try his views of streamlining trams and buses. Incidentally he said, "It costs the same whether to design an austere or attractive vehicle". At this point he luckily met William Lockhart Marshall of the English Electric Company at Preston, who had similar ideas and contributed greatly to planning the rail-coach, which was the first of the new fleet. Much of the planning was done on our dining room table. "Mac" became a great friend, and eventually helped design the new Coronations twenty years later.

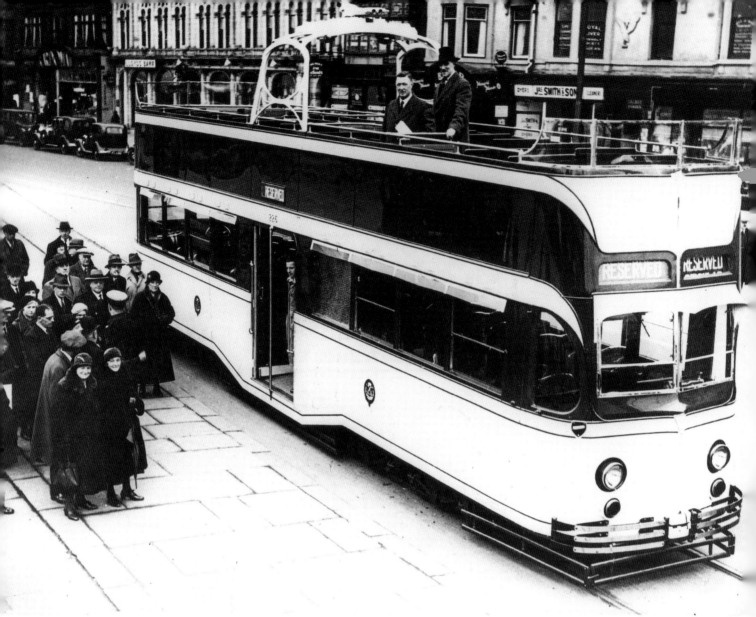

"Luxury Dreadnought"226 for inspection by the public in January1934 at North Pier. Twelve more were ordered and had more sloped fronts, and with 226 became 237 – 249, now 700 – 712. (Gazette)

The "Five Year Plan" opened with the new rail-coach, which was designed for the seaside resort of Blackpool, and not for the inland towns. He felt that the exceptional traffic must have its own class of rolling-stock, in order to give credit to the town. On 19th June 1933 the first rail-coach came from English Electric as a trial. Numbered 200 it was shown to the delegates of the Municipal Tramway Conference in Blackpool, and caused great excitement. Photographs appeared in the press all over the World, including London, Sudan, Rotterdam, Melbourne and many others. In January 1934, the prototype open "Boat" and open-top streamliner called "Luxury Dreadnought" were displayed on the siding at North Pier. The Transport Committee, having ordered 24 rail-coaches decided to order another 11 Boats and 12 open-top streamliners. These were followed by fourteen enclosed double-deckers christened "Balloons" in 1935, along with 20 more E.E. rail-coaches in 1936 and 20 railcars by Brush in 1937. By 1938 the fleet was completely modernised - apart from the Marton route - with the 104 new trams running on the Promenade and causing admiration. There were also double-deck buses with centre-entrances and open single-deck runabouts. Incidentally there is a sculpture of the double-decker bus seen on the wall panel of the Town Hall today. There was now a reduced claim for accidents because the centre entrances prevented passengers from jumping on or off the back platforms of both buses and trams. Having catered for vast numbers of visitors during Lancashire Wakes Weeks, Blackpool Transport was ready for the huge influx of R.A.F., Civil Servants, evacuees from London and American G.I.s with the outbreak of the Second World War.

WALTER LUFF - CIVIL DEFENCE TRANSPORT OFFICER - 1939-45

We returned early from a holiday in Oban, when declaration of war was expected on 3rd September 1939. Walter Luff was made Civil Defence Transport Officer and had a blue and gold arm-band, which was later embroidered for him by one of his staff. He was then in charge of Auxiliary Ambulances and Mobile Canteens, which had to be kept in tip top order, in case they were ever needed. In actual fact, although there were frequent Air Raid warnings, the German Luftwaffe just took their bearings for bombing Barrow shipyards from the three Blackpool piers. Only one lot of bombs was dropped on the North Station area in September 1940, during the return of the bombers from a raid on Barrow. My father and other Civil Defence officials were examining the damage, and the next day two unexploded bombs were found where they had landed. Each evening as the War progressed, there were telephone calls giving warnings about approaching enemy aircraft. These took the form of; "Yellow warning Sir", Purple warning Sir" or "Red warning Sir." He had to set off back to the depot for purple or red warnings, and he wore a tin-hat with an "A" and three black diamonds marked on it. He had petrol for his car to drive on Civil Defence and A.R.P work, and also to drive on any bus or tram routes to inspect them. However he could not go over the town boundaries by car. The main problems for Blackpool were mines, and wherever one was sighted, the lifeboat had to be moved across to Rigby Road depot to keep it safe. Once a mine was sighted floating on the sea and approaching the promenade near to the Cenotaph, and thus the Lifeboat Committee Chairman Ald. Tatham and the crew were called out. The two men who dealt with mines were elsewhere, so the crew launched the lifeboat and threw a net over the mine and towed it out of sight of the land. They then shot at it and when it eventually exploded, the lifeboat went up in the air and landed upside down in the sea. Fortunately it was self-righting, but all the crew and Ald Tatham were soaked!

A small boy admires the imposing tram at Squires Gate, appealing for the War Weapons Week and with a model Spitfire mounted at each end. This was introduced as illuminated-car"Bandwagon" in 1937, and as illuminated-car "Progress"in 1949. (Gazette)

The crew of Bandwagon demonstrate gas-masks. Wartime women platform-staff in uniform in 1940.

He enrolled women from his offices to drive the ambulances and canteens, and 300 men in the Transport Department trained in various sections of A.R.P. work. I have also seen a photograph of drivers and conductors with wooden guns. To achieve camouflage he changed the livery of buses and trams to mainly green on the lower panels and roofs, so that cream colour did not show by moonlight, especially if there was a full moon. In July 1940, 38 women conductresses were employed, who had white piping on their uniforms, because the men who had green piping on their uniforms, wanted them to be distinctive. Conductress skirts soon changed to trousers, especially when climbing stairs on the double-deckers. Incidentally, Walter Luff was the only Manager in the country to have two Spitfires in his Department, since two which were bought by funds raised by the people of Blackpool, mistakenly carried the Blackpool Corporation Transport circular badge, while fighting battles! Blackpool was overflowing with R.A.F. airmen, Polish troops and G.I.s from America, so record takings resulted, especially on the trams which fortunately did not use petrol or rubber-tyres. These record takings increased each year, and with the fare of 1d per mile the aim was to always have another tram in sight. Certainly many thousands of pounds were taken for rate-relief, against the wishes of my father.

WALTER LUFF - AFTER THE WAR 1945-1954

In 1945 my father was made President of the Light Railway Transport League, which had been founded in 1938 to advocate the developments of tramways throughout Britain. Clearly they felt that Walter Luff had been successful in achieving this in Blackpool. However in 1947 he persuaded Blackpool Council to vote in favour of relaying the Marton route and introduce modern trams. In 1949 he received the Gold Medal from the Institute of Transport, in recognition of his success here. He also thought that trams would one day be museum pieces along with steam engines, and so he saved old trams at the back of the depots, saying that one day there would be a tram museum, ideally at Bispham depot. This would be at the other end of the system from the Pleasure Beach, so that enthusiasts would travel by tram between the two. He also said that the life of a tramcar was twenty years, and so in post-war years he started a plan for the replacement of the 1933-39 fleet. He heard that Stockholm had a new type of tram and he suggested to the Corporation that himself and "experts" on his staff should go to Stockholm to look at them. However the Corporation said that the proposed trip would be too expensive, because the return journey by rail and sea would cost £39-12s-9d each. He then asked tram enthusiasts everywhere to send him designs for twenty new trams, saying that he did not mind what they looked like, so long as they impressed holiday-makers and kept

(Above) A busy scene at Royal Oak, with South Station and Palladium Cinema in post-war years, served by two Standard trams and a Leyland Tiger bus on route 10. Undoubtedly, Walter Luff saved the Marton route by persuading the Council to vote for track-relaying on 8th January 1947.

(Below) A nostalgic scene in Church Street, with Standard 48 passing a Marton "Vambac" on 28th October 1962, the last day of the route. (Author's Collection)

The inaugural journey of Coronation 304 on June 16th 1952, with Walter Luff in the cab instructing the Mayor in how to operate the controls as it moves over the crossover through the crowd. (Gazette)

up the profits. However it would maintain the town's reputation for having the world's most original tramcars, while passengers getting off and on quickly was what mattered most. However no suitable designs emerged and so he and "Mac" Marshall designed the twenty-five new Coronation cars. This time they were built by Charles Roberts of Horbury, since English Electric of Preston now were producing fighter aircraft like the Lightning.

When the Coronations were completed, there was more controversy about their width and whether they would go round the corner in the town centre. They were not intended to operate on inland routes, but on the Promenade route from Starr Gate to Fleetwood. However some Councillors insisted that one was tried from Talbot Square to Marton, via the sharp curve from Clifton Street to Abingdon Street. There was a lot of publicity in the Gazette, and several Councillors decided to follow Coronation 305 in their cars. In the paper it said that Walter Luff was on board with other V.I.Ps, but in fact he was at home with his family. Late in the evening on 6th August 1952 the phone rang and it was Jack

Coronation 305 at Devonshire Square after midnight, upon its return from Marton depot for the first and last time... (Gazette)

Parkinson - Traffic Superintendant - ringing from the phone box outside the G.P.O.. He said: "It's alright sir, she's round the corner". My father just said: "Thank you", and rang off. My mother thought he ought to have shown some feeling of relief and pleasure, but he said: "Oh I knew she'd go round, she's been round the curve before. Mr.Bellhouse took her round a fortnight ago, at 2 a.m. in the morning." This was a well-kept secret!

There is still a mistaken belief that my father asked to stay on after retirement age in order to see the introduction of the Coronations, this is not true! In 1952 the Transport Committee regarded incredulously that he was reaching retirement age, so they decided to recommend to the Council to retain his services on a year-to-year basis. In the Evening Gazette of 1953 it stated: "Their regard for his managerial achievements is such that they would like to retain his services as long as possible". In fact he hoped to continue until he was 70, as his father had done. However in March 1954 Ald.Tatham died, he had been Transport Committee Chairman for many years, and had always been a stalwart champion and supporter of the General Manager. His death shocked my father, along with his next medical which diagnosed he had diabetes, so he thought he must be really ill. These two factors made him decide to retire, and thus he retired on 20th June 1954, and moved to Scalby near Scarborough. Looking back at Blackpool after his retirement, he knew there were adverts on the trams but he had not expected that his Balloons would lose their appearance by what he called "carbuncles" to the front of them, replacing the twin indicators. Therefore he never went back to Blackpool again, even when he was invited to the 75th Anniversary of the Tramway in 1960. After this and the closure of the street routes, the four historic trams were given to Crich N.T.M. in January 1963. Then Chaceley Humpidge - Manager of Sheffield Transport & President of T.M.S - invited my father to see them in the early years of the Museum. Certainly he sat on crossbench car 2, which was saved along with 4 from 1885, Dreadnought 59, and Box 40 all those years ago. He died on 17th February 1969 aged 81, and was buried at Pickering in North Yorkshire. I am glad that today he undoubtedly remains part of Blackpool Tramway's history!

One of the 1935 "Gondola" buses 114 – 119, seen here passing Central Station and in front of Feldmans Theatre which was the tram terminus until 1936.

(Right) Walter Luff is seen upstairs on a Leyland Titan bus, demonstrating to the Transport Commitee the speaker for the driver to announce the stops. Notice the opening roof panel, and Alhambrinal. (Daphne Luff)

PROLOGUE OF J.C. FRANKLIN - GENERAL MANAGER 1954-1974

It is interesting to recall Joe Franklin's memories of his career in Transport, when I met him after his retirement on 21st June 1975. During his time as General Manager of Blackpool Transport, he did correspond with me as an enthusiast, having asked him about the latest developments on the tramway. However I did first meet him in 1959 in Copse Road depot, while a friend and myself were exploring the upper-deck of the Dreadnought. We came down the twin staircases to the platform, and were confronted by the imposing figure of Mr. Franklin. He asked what we were doing there, and I was able to produce his letter of permission, and he did smile. In the same year I was a point-boy at Central Station terminus, and I frequently saw him at lunchtime when he used to travel by tram from Manchester Square and arrive there to survey the busy scene of trams reversing and loading. I always politely greeted him, but he only nodded in response, boarded the next tram and left in the driver's cab at the controls. Generally speaking Managers were involved in the administrative aspect of Transport, but J.C.Franklin wanted to keep in touch with reality. He was essentially a dynamic character, and thus the appearance of the prototype twin-car 276-275 on its trial run to Fleetwood in 1958, forecast the appearance of ten new trailers in 1960. Then the 75th Anniversary of the Tramway, with the restoration of four historic trams previously saved by Walter Luff, led the two processions on 29th September 1960. They were also used on Promenade Circulars, which provided a big attraction for the holiday-makers. The creation of five new illuminated trams between 1959 and 1965 provided real tours of the Illuminations, and provided mobile attractions for the scene. While this contrasted with the closure of the street tramway routes 1961-63, new developments stressed the importance of the Promenade and Fleetwood route. Finally, his creation of the thirteen OMOs ensured that there would be more economic operation than the expensive Coronations. Therefore he was undoubtedly a good Transport Manager for Blackpool over twenty years, and thus he became known as "Showman of the Trams".

In 1959 the first post-war Illuminated tram "Blackpool Belle" was created from Toastrack 163, is seen here outside the Works and flying two suitable flags. (Author's Collection)

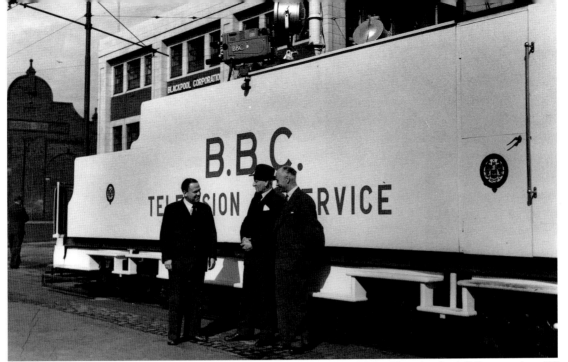

Television tram 166 for the BBC outside the Transport Office with General Manager J.C.Franklin and senior staff. You cannot see 165 which contained a generator. In 1956 the two Toastracks were built first for BBC and then ATV.

INTERVIEW WITH J.C. FRANKLIN AFTER HIS RETIREMENT 21st JUNE 1975

I was the Chief Engineer at Salford from 1946 to 1951, and we had two tram routes 70 and 71, which provided the Docks circular in each direction. Altogether there were 57 trams, but I was lucky to get 15 on service. Some of the drivers used to swing the controller-handle right round when they were outside Frederick Road depot to deliberately burn-out the motors. Because there were no spare cars serviceable, this meant that they could take the rest of the day off. I therefore arranged that two cars were parked outside the dept as stand-by cars ready to take-over when this happened. What the driver did not know was that these cars were quite incapable of running! The buses were also in appalling condition, and when I arrived I noticed that some had "8" painted on the side. "What does that mean?" I asked the foreman. "Oh, the number "8" is the joint route to Bolton", he replied. "These are the only buses that will get there and back". Only a few days after arriving in Salford, Manager Charles Baroth and I had to visit the Traffic Commissioners, and the first thing he said to me was: "Mr.Franklin, I don't know whether your predecessor told you this, but we have issued a warning that unless Salford buses improve radically within six months, we will take over the undertaking. You could find yourself looking for another job". I went back to the depot and worked for day and night to improve at least some of the buses. There was no large-scale improvement, but we wanted to show that at least we were trying. We got a few of the buses looking respectable, though the rest were as bad as ever.

I was appointed Rochdale Manager in 1951, and then Blackpool in 1954. I am a Lancashire man and I liked Blackpool, so that there was not another undertaking that I would like to run more. Walter Luff should have retired in 1952 when he was 65. I was worried about this because I wanted the Blackpool job, but with only one year's experience as a Manager, I would stand no chance. When I learned that Walter was to stay on for a year and then for two years, this gave me a chance. When the job was advertised then I applied. Many members of the Transport Association did not apply, because the job had been black-listed since the salary was too low at £1,500, and at Rochdale I was already on £1,600. At the Committee Room, Rhodes Marshall was the Chairman of the appointment board. One of the Committee members asked why my operating costs were much higher than Blackpool's. I said "Indeed they are, but look at your revenue per mile, and you will see that my profit is much higher than yours. You see, Walter Luff has had a very intensive service but with a very high mileage, and while this brought his operating costs down". However, trams were never mentioned at this interview. I was appointed at £1,750, and started on July 15th 1954. After a year, I was astonished to be given an increase of £500, which Rhodes Marshall had arranged for me.

MY BLACKPOOL EXPERIENCE

My first weeks in Blackpool were an eye-opener, and I was soon wondering what sort of job I had come to. I knew Walter Luff, but I only had one meeting with him before I took over. I then asked him two questions: "You have bought one hundred buses from Burlinghams and you still owe them a lot of money. I can't see from the accounts where you are going to get this money from?" "There's nothing to worry about", said Walter, and that was all I could get out of him. The second question was about the new Coronation trams: "I know you are having a lot of trouble with your new trams"."No, there's no trouble". "But I know there is, because I have been told by your suppliers"."Well we've had a bit of trouble, but nothing serious". He took me into the Works, and it had been the first time he had been in there for four years. While were in there, Works Manager Clarke came up and said; "Mr. Luff, I've got fourteen Coronations off the road". Walter Luff whipped me out of there like lightning!

The main trouble of the Coronations was the bearings which were not strong enough, because these trams were much heavier. Representatives of Maley & Taunton and Charles Roberts were called in to see what could be done. Under the threat of legal action, new bearings were made by Maley & Taunton and £1,000 was given by Charles Roberts towards the cost of sealing the leaking roof-windows. I got Maley & Taunton to fit new bearings free-of-charge, which was quite an expense for them. They cost £14 each, there were eight on each tram therefore £112 per car, and for 25 trams it cost £2,800. The faulty-bearings and the rubber sandwiches in the wheels put great strain on the axles, and they broke regularly. On several occasions the press-on wheels actually fell off, though fortunately it happened when the cars were starting or stopping. In my view the Spivs were therefore the World's worst buy, they cost totally £300,000 or really £500,000 when you add the loan-charges. However, just before buying them, £300,000 was taken out of the Transport reserves and otherwise used. We were constantly modifying them to maintain their safe-operation, many dewirements were caused by 6-inch swivel-heads mounted on a 20-foot trolley, causing a "whipping" action. Incidentally, Walter Luff assured the Transport Committee that the Spivs could run on the Marton route, and so

Coronation 316 in 1955, having been rebuilt with a new covered-roof, closed standee-windows and without chrome beading. It is interesting to see its destination, NORTH STATION BLACKPOOL which was not visited by Coronation cars. (W.R.Buckley)

Early in 1958 the prototype twin-car 276+275 at North Pier is demonstrating the loading-technique, using members of staff including Manager J.C. Franklin at the door of 275. Being fresh from the Works they are painted all-cream, but not yet lined green and numbered. (E.R. Hargreaves)

they insisted on a demonstration. The main problem was the sharp curve in front of the G.P.O., where there were no parking restrictions, and the length of the new cars could have hit the parked-cars there. Astutely Walter arranged the trial-run at midnight and ensured that there were no parked-cars on this curve. He did not run 305 any further than Marton depot, as there might have been a problem on the South Station bridge. Thus I ruled that the Coronations would only be used on the Starr Gate to Fleetwood route. It is in my view that these trams had been bought with the idea of replacing the double-decker Balloons, which had not a penny spent on them for years. Consequently I started by putting them back in order, increasing their capacity from 84 to 94 and having larger single-indicators installed. I was a bit worried about the extra ten passengers upstairs might affect the tilting of the car, but fortunately there was no tilt-test for trams!

Nostalgic scenes of Boats on the Circular Tour at Starr Gate and in Squires Gate Lane. Notice the junction of the track for blue-cars going to Lytham St.Annes until 1936. (Steve Palmer)

(Left) 276-T6 at Fleetwood Ferry in cream livery. (Right) 277 reversing in Harrowside at Easter 1963. (Steve Palmer)

A MAN OF ACTION!

I was astonished to find that the double-deckers had never run to Fleetwood, and on enquiring from the Ministry of Transport, I was told that the check-rails would be needed to stop them overturning. So we bolted on miles of angle-iron which would not have stopped a tram turning over, but satisfied the Ministry of Transport. Therefore on 1st July 1958 a Balloon in the green livery and showing "1 - FLEETWOOD" on its twin indicators, set out from North Station for the first time. There was a sequel to this many years later, when Lt.Col. McNaughton inspected the first of the OMO trams in 1972. The inspector was most enthusiastic about trams and drove the new tram all the way to Fleetwood. He noticed the angle-iron bolted to the track and asked why it was there. When we told him, he said that it was quite unnecessary, and we later received a letter from the M. of T. to confirm it. In the late Fifties many people suggested that we buy second-hand trams from systems which were closing-down, and I paid a visit to Aberdeen to inspect their centre-entrance cars. They were short and narrow-gutted making the inside saloons look very cramped, and not fast enough for us. I also went unofficially to Leeds and went out with Manager Mr. Findlay on Leeds 602, the all-electric car with VAMBAC equipment. It was small and too powerful for Blackpool, which would have blown our sub-stations, as did the Coronations originally.

(Left) Many passengers boarding 700 in North Albert Street, notice its reversed indicator display-box. (Right) Central Promenade in 1977 with OMO 2 and followed by 676 - 686, renumbered in 1968. (Steve Palmer)

75th Anniversary 1960

(Above) An interesting sight of 2 & 40 at Station Road terminus during 1960.

(Above) "This Is It" - the first three of the procession at Little Bispham in September 1960.

(Above) July 1960 on a memorable tour with 2 & 59 in Pharos Street, Fleetwood.

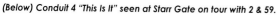

(Below) Conduit 4 "This Is It" seen at Starr Gate on tour with 2 & 59.

(Below) Final tour on Dreadnought 59 in January 1963, followed by a railcoach and its driver here on South Promenade. (Authors Collection)

The old illuminated cars Gondola and Lifeboat were practically "live", and they were a nightmare to us whenever it rained and they were carrying passengers. It is a miracle that nobody was electrocuted! We used to charge a special fare to ride on them, and people asked why did they pay more than the ordinary Tour of the Illuminations. In 1959 I decided to put illuminations on two of the Standard cars 158 & 159, and then created the "Blackpool Belle" to replace the old "Progress" car. When it was new, Jayne Mansfield performed the switch-on of the Illuminations, and Publicity officer Harry Porter and I decided that it would be a nice idea to seat the guests at the front of the Belle, for a tour of the Lights. Unfortunately the Mayor Ald. Machin was somewhat corpulent, and when he tried to reach the seats by squeezing through the gangway, his evening-jacket buttons were torn off. There were similar problems for the shapely Miss Mansfield! The "Rocket" followed in 1961 and the "Western Train" in 1962, from an idea by my wife who saw an American railroad locomotive on the television. This was followed by the "Hovertram" in 1963, and frigate "H.M.S. Blackpool" in 1965, starting a new generation of illuminated trams.

Right from square-one, I knew that the street routes would eventually have to go. The track on Lytham Road was unsafe, much of it being pre-war, and Dickson Road had foundation-trouble. I thought that the Marton route should not have been relaid in 1948, and the Marton Vambacs needed much maintenance. The cost of spare parts for the Spivs was becoming astronomic, especially the rubber sandwiches because of the small quantities involved. Once the loan was repaid in 1968, we started to get rid of the Coronations with 313. We converted half of them to have ordinary E.E. Z6 controllers, in order to keep them running. Spare parts from the scrapped Marton cars were of little use, as there was not much inter-changeability between the two. Regarding change of directions, if I had tried to build a one-man tram in 1958, it would not have stood a chance, but after the one-man buses had been introduced, the climate was different. We rebuilt Brush-car 638, but that was no good from the start, because the passenger-door was behind the driver and we had to move the resistances on the roof. This was really a false start, but when we started planning the OMOs, we set up a weekly committee and kept

A special display of the Western Train locomotive on the traverser and in front of the Works buildings in 1963, built out of English Electric railcoach 209. Subsequently restored and rebuilt from 677 in 2009. (Studio D)

(Above) Standard 40 is the final service car from Talbot Square. (R.P. Fergusson)

them involved in what we were doing. Thus we never had a bit of trouble with the unions, who were involved. The drastic step of changing the position of the controller to drive as a right-hander, was accepted straight away. After we provided the 13 OMOs for the service, I suggested in a report that the Boats should be used for further conversions, and possibly the two disused double-deckers 714 and 725. The Brush-cars were not suitable because of the design of the frames, and with bounce-and-roll movements on E.M.B. bogies. Undoubtedly by this time the climate of the Council was increasingly hostile to the tramway, and thus the Management had to take drastic measures to secure the future of the Promenade and Fleetwood lines. Therefore Chief Engineer Alan Williams and myself struggled to make the trams economic, hence the introduction of the OMOs and the phasing-out of the Coronations with their expensive running-costs. By the time of my retirement in 1974, with one-man operation established and costs reduced, the future was more secure!

Two final nights of the street routes (left) Standard 48 arrives at Marton Depot from Royal Oak on 28th October 1962. (Steve Palmer) (right) Balloon 256 is about to leave North Station on 27th October 1963 for Cabin, and its former Tramroad driver Tom Leeming is standing in front of it. (Peter Fitton)

PROLOGUE OF DEREK HYDE, GENERAL MANAGER 1974 -1986

by Author Steve Palmer

The change of General Manager in 1974 coincided with Local Government Reorganisation, which provided an opportunity for Derek Hyde - a Lancashire man - to leave Coventry City Transport, which was being absorbed into West Midlands PTE, and come to Blackpool. It is interesting to identify the tramway developments during his time, and certainly as an engineer Derek Hyde was known for visiting the Works and discussing progress on the trams with the staff. His arrival was also welcome in the sense that his brother Geof Hyde was Chairman of the National Tramway Museum, and indeed became President in the Blackpool Centenary Year 1985. Thus the Hyde brothers were seen together at tramway events in Blackpool in that year, albeit each in different capacities! Undoubtedly Derek Hyde's time as General Manager was notable for upgrading the tramway fleet, commencing with the Jubilee double-deckers and continuing with the Centenary cars to replace the O.M.O.s. A new truck and suspension system was designed by the Department for these cars and a major development was Installed with the new technology of electronic "Chopper" control, made by the Brush Company. However, the Centenary of the Tramway in 1985 was the most memorable event on September 29th with the procession of twenty trams led by the 1885 car 4, and including trams from six different tramway systems. I well remember meeting Derek Hyde and his wife at the end of the Centenary Day, being appropriately dressed in Victorian costume, and he said that it had been a most successful day, especially riding on the open-top of the 1885 tram at the head of the procession. In the following year, Derek Hyde stood down as the General Manager, since the Municipal Transport Department became Blackpool Transport Services, and he became a consultant. Undoubtedly, his time as General Manager maintained the spirit of "Progress" for the tramway.

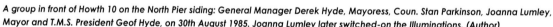

A group in front of Howth 10 on the North Pier siding: General Manager Derek Hyde, Mayoress, Coun. Stan Parkinson, Joanna Lumley, Mayor and T.M.S. President Geof Hyde, on 30th August 1985. Joanna Lumley later switched-on the Illuminations. (Author)

(Above) 678 fitted with the Brecknell-Willis pantograph in 1975 at depot. (Right) June 1976, OMO 5 having lost its collector-plate, outside the Tower. (Author)

EVENTS OF TWELVE TRAMWAY YEARS 1974 - 1986

From detailed notes kept by the Author

Towards the end of 1974 it was significant that OMO 9 went into service as the last in the "plum and custard" livery. However, the significance of 1975 was the fact that the Fleetwood service was operated by the OMOs throughout the season, although double-deck Balloons operated on selected routes only during the peak weeks of the summer season. Ironically, the last five of the Coronation cars were in use, but more significantly OMO 10 entered service, painted in the new red and cream livery to identify it for passengers paying their fares to the driver. Likewise 11 & 12 followed in May and June, but 10 was known by the staff as "Bouncing Bessie", thanks to its METALASTIK bogie suspension. Another claim to fame was towing-car 678, which was fitted with the first of the Brecknell & Willis power-collector, and operated only between Cleveleys and Starr Gate. It was not able to use the Pleasure Beach loop because the overhead needed re-aligning at the curves. In Fleetwood, the Ferry curves were temporarily fitted with double-wires for separate use of trolleys and pantographs. However the testing of this overhead was undertaken first by Engineering car 754, which had the collector mounted on its overhead platform and made a trial run to Fleetwood on 4th June 1975, thus enabling 678 to visit the location. Incidentally, this 754 is now rebuilt as open-top 31 and operates at Beamish.

(Below) OMO 10 at Manchester Square with "LOOK OUT TRAMS ABOUT" sign. (Author)

The newly-restored Dreadnought 59 returning to the depot after the Borough Centenary procession. (Author)

1976 - RETURN OF THE DREADNOUGHT

At this time, advertising boxes were fitted on OMOs 2, 4, 6, 7, 8, together with Brush-cars 623, 626, 677, 631 & 637, on which they look too long, having come from the withdrawn Coronation cars. However, the more interesting development was the preparation of drawings for a new double-decker, which would be 46 feet in length, with the bogie mounting moved out. The entrance would be at the front and fixed bus seating used, with half facing forward and half backwards, eliminating the traditional swing-over seats. It was planned for the reconstruction of Balloon 725, which at that time was stripped-down in Blundell Street depot. It was also to be fitted with a remote-control system and designs were being prepared at G.E.C., Trafford Park, Manchester. However, work did not begin until 26th October 1976, when 725 was moved into the Works Body Shop. Certainly 1976 was significant for the Centenary of Blackpool Borough, and the Civic Trust in 1975 had sponsored the return of the Dreadnought, which was on display on the Promenade at Foxhall, before going to the Technical College for restoration. It returned to the rails on Friday 22 May 1976, and first travelled along the Promenade on 29th May. It was specially filmed on the historic track in Princess Street on 3rd June, as a prelude to the Centenary Procession on Saturday 12th June, when 59 stood opposite the Tower with Civic Trust members in period costumes. Subsequently they went for a ride to the Pleasure Beach, after which the public like myself could ride to Bispham and back to the depot. Undoubtedly this was quite a thrill, being on 59 for the first time since 1965. I noticed that the panel lining was not quite complete, and that it carried adverts for Derbyshire's Bread and Pleasure Beach on its display boards. Therefore, once again the famous Dreadnought had become part of the Blackpool scene, and actually survived here until 1990.

In the tramway scene that year, the final Brush-car 621 which still had its twin indicators looked better than the rebuilt ones with single-indicators. A dramatic scene took place outside the Tower on 8th June, when OMO 5 broke its Brecknell Willis collector and brought down a section of the overhead. I remember the large collector-plate laying on the promenade behind the tram, and luckily it did not hit any pedestrians. The tower-wagon came and restored the overhead, then pulling 5 back to the depot where it was fitted with a trolley. In the same month the final OMO 13 was seen on trial, with a rope attached to its pantograph in case of emergency with its A/c alternator. Down at the depot in August, I saw four remaining Coronation cars which were due to be removed soon. 655, 661, 662 would go to the scrap merchant, while 663 had been bought by Graham Oliver, a young enthusiast. On 19th August I watched it being lifted by two cranes on to a lorry-

(Left) Coronation 663 being loaded for its trip to Lytham. (Right) Brush-car 621 in its original style. (Author)

trailer, I followed it along Lytham Road, Squires Gate Lane and Clifton Drive to Lytham Creek Railway. When it was unloaded 660 was pulled along the track by a steam engine making an unusual sight! However it suffered from flooding here, and was moved to Bradford Transport Museum, then to St. Helens Transport Museum in company with 304, and now it is at the local Marton L.T.T. museum.

BOAT 603 - THE MOST TRAVELLED TRAM

In that year it was most interesting to record all the appearance and usage of the fleet. Certainly the most significant absentee was Boat 603, which had been sent to Philadelphia U.S.A. to help with the celebration of the Bi-Centenary of the city. It had to be re-gauged to 5ft 3ins, and repainted in white and orange with colour flares round the panels. Together with several other vintage trams borrowed from U.S.A. museums, 603 gave rides through the historic city centre. Whereas 603 returned to Blackpool in 1978, it never again ran here because of its need for re-gauging. However, it returned again to U.S.A. in 1985, where it has since operated in San Fransisco Trolley Festival, thus being our most travelled tram!

Boat-car 603 seen on 5th Street in Philadelphia, in its special Bi-Centenary livery for the U.S.A. city. (Ian M. Dougill)

Easter 1981 with a scene at Norbreck, as 678 tows OMO 5 with a broken pantograph back to the depot. (Author)

Regarding the fleet at home, six Boats were in use and all 13 OMOs, of which 2, 3, 4, 5, 13 bogies had METALASTIK suspension. Of the Brush-cars, several were painted in different styles, including 622 as the Zoo tram, with a tiger's face on each end, 634 in Centenary Anniversary livery and 638 was all-white as the experimental OMO tram, now having a crew of two. Unfortunately 629 stood derelict in Blundell Street depot, together with 635 which was to be preserved for the National Tram Museum. It left Blackpool for Mode Wheel workshop in Salford on 14th March 1977, where it was restored to 1937 original style with sliding roofs from railcoach 220. Subsequently it was taken to N.T.M. Crich in September 2005, and we hope that it will operate there one day. At this time some of the Brush-cars still had original roof-windows: 624, 625, 629, 635, 636, 637 & 638, and all service cars had fan-heaters in each saloon. Of the twin-cars 671 - 677 were permanently linked to their trailers and thus could be driven from trailers 681- 687, but 678 - 680 operated separately, thus leaving trailers 688 - 690 disused in the depot. Of the Balloons, 709, 714, 717, 722 still had double-indicators, and 714, 715, 720 & 722 had the original capacity of 84. Coronation 660 remained in the fleet and together with Dreadnought 59 both were used for Illumination tours and on Promenade specials, thus totalling 85 trams in the fleet. At this time there was concern about the condition of OMOs, and I remember being shown the cracked bogie frame of OMO 2 and the saloon floor of OMO 3 from underneath, which was being cut by the wheels. This was caused by the sagging long body-frame hitting the wheels. By the end of the year work had started on 725, with its end being removed and new extension of its frame fitted, thus changing its appearance as a new double-decker 761.

(Below) Little Bispham with OMO 5, 708 & 707 on a tour for the L.R.T.A. in October 1975. (Author)

622 at Starr Gate showing the new Zoo advertising livery in October 1975, being the first in this style. (Author)

ROYAL JUBILEE YEAR 1977

In this year the Tower was painted silver to indicate the celebration of the Queen's Silver Jubilee and Brush-car 634 was modified for this occasion. During the winter work took place on relaying the track of Central Promenade, and early in 1977 work started in relaying South Promenade which took place between Harrowside and Pleasure Beach. In those days rail was delivered to Thornton Gate sidings, and collected by 624 and trailer which delivered it to the relaying site. I remember that 18 pairs of street rail was relaid in four weeks by the track-gang. The 1977 summer service from 1st July comprised 25 route cards: routes 1 - 9 were OMO operated, 10 - 23 Balloon operated, and 101 - 102 as Promenade "specials". This provided a five minute headway between Starr Gate & Little Bispham, and 10 minute headway to Fleetwood. Routes 1 - 9 operated the Fleetwood route from 5 - 50 onwards, routes 10 - 23 started with a round-trip Manchester Square - Little Bispham - Starr Gate, and then the Balloons went on to Fleetwood service for the whole day until 1800 to 1930 in the evening. Market Day on Tuesday had always been the busiest day, when up to 55 trams were in use over the system, including six twin-cars on the Fleetwood route as "specials". Of course, the Boats were always seen on the Promenade, providing the weather was good. At this time it was rather sad to see Rossall siding de-wired, on the excuse of needing more overhead wiring, but the siding eventually disappeared, removing its wartime evidence of troops coming here by tram.

Balloon 707 seen at Starr Gate, advertising Empire Pools in the first whole-tram advertising in 1975. (Author)

THE APEARANCE OF JUBILEE CAR 761

Inside the Body Shop , work on 725 - to become Jubilee-car 761 - was proceeding by August 1977 so that the car was fitted with large window frames and was panelled completely along one side. The general appearance with the new rectangular ends made it look like a Liverpool Atlantean bus, since the ends of the roof were arched in the centre. At the time, it was estimated that the car would seat 110 passengers on fixed bus-type seating, but in reality it became 98 seats to allow more movement for passengers. When I went to the upper saloon, I found that it looked almost complete with plastic wood-grain panelling under the windows, and a white plastic ceiling with continuous bell-strips along the full length of the car, together with eight fluorescent light-fittings. The lower saloon was still unfinished, since there was delay on deciding on the control system. In fact G.E.C. proved too expensive for its electro-pneumatic system, while Westinghouse were currently offering "chopper control" system which would be operated by a control-stick at each end and equipment fitted under the stairs. The new bogies were still in pieces in the Fitting Shop, having to be rebuilt with a bolster suspension. Engineer Stuart Pillar was anxious to get the whole job right before putting it in service, and the estimates were that it would take another six months yet. However, in February 1978 the trial bogies were put under 708, and I heard that on its trial run to Fleetwood, the car appeared to bounce while crossing point-work, which thus needed modification. The roll-out of 761 took place at 8-20 on 19th April 1979, pulled by the Diamond "T". It looked very handsome in the new livery, but I noticed it swaying from side to side as it crossed the depot points, showing the suspension. 680 pushed it into the Fitting Shop, where it was fitted with the alternator and a small pantograph on four posts However, it was 4th June 1979 that 761 was taken on trial to Fleetwood, following its inspection by the Railway Inspector, and passed for driver training. I remember that 761 looked very imposing for the watching passengers, but they were first able to board it on 2nd July 1979 when it went into service, driven by Jim Shearer, who also happened to be F.T.S. Chairman!

At the time, I used to find it interesting to hear the comments of the engineering staff, for example I was told that stored 714 would be rebuilt like 761, but it would have two doorways to facilitate passenger movement. Also it was going to be investigated that a firm could assemble parts of new bodies for Balloons to be rebuilt, and assembled in Blundell Street depot, but this never happened. Eric Dyson - the Works Manager - told me that mistakes were made in the past, by making non standard Illuminated cars, like the Rocket and Frigate built from Pantographs cars 168 and 170, having Witton (WT28L) motors and thus larger 30 inch wheels. He also commented that mistakes were made in the Sixties by scrapping the English Electric railcoaches, and keeping the non-standard Brush cars. For example he recalled when 626 was in the paint shop, it was found to be completely

Two views of 761 in January 1980, as it poses in front of the Transport Office and historic Blundell Street depot. 761 looks handsome in this livery, which was also seen on Atlantean buses. (Author)

Face-to-face for two Balloons 705 and 706, which collided at Pleasure Beach loop, owing to south-bound points left open for loop-line, and thus turned 705 into the approaching 706 from Starr Gate. Here 712 is about to pull 705 back to the depot, and it was never seen in service again! (Gazette)

rotten at one end, and had to be rebuilt, and Brush cars were also re-equipped with E.E. equipment. In 1980, it is worth recording developments which took place, notably the breaking-up of Brush-car 629 and rebuilding of 621 without its traditional twin indicators. Fortunately 761 had a trouble-free season, but a decision was made about the rebuilding of 714 and thus construction materials had been ordered, including new ends, and it was hoped that work would start in January 1981. The Fitting-shop was now making its own diamond-shaped pantographs, to replace trolleys. In July 1980 Balloons 705 & 706 had a head-on collision at Pleasure Beach, owing to a set of points left open. While 705 was scrapped in Blundell Street depot in 1982, 706 was rebuilt as an original open-topper in 1985 for the Centenary. Regarding rebuilding 714 to 762, I understood that new bogies were to be built by a local engineering firm, and that new equipment by Brush would cost twice as much as that in 761. Also it was interesting that investigating was taking place into future new trams.

BOLTON 66 JOINS THE FLEET

During the winter on 22 November 1980, there was a match between Blackpool & Fleetwood football teams, and so there were football specials on the tramway for the first time since the Sixties. Thus four Balloons - 701, 707, 712, 713 - operated from the Ferry at 1300, showing PLEASURE BEACH on their blinds, unloaded the supporters at St.Chads stop and returned to the depot. At 1645 when the match was over - the score was Blackpool 4 - Fleetwood 0 - the four Balloons turned at the Pleasure Beach and picked up the supporters at St.Chads for their return to Fleetwood. Dreadnought 59 was hired to carry the Fleetwood football team, and correctly showed FOOTBALL GROUND on its indicators. Certainly these trams used to be football specials along Central Drive until

Bolton 66 seen at Bispham Top on its first tour to Fleetwood in 1981. (Author)

1934. However 1981 began by Boat 600 fitted with one of the new pantographs made by Blackpool Transport. The carbon running-surface would last as long as six bronze trolley-wheels, and so I thought that this year might be the end of trolleys, but it was not. Behind the scenes, progress on 762 was rapid, and Engineer Stuart Pillar told me that a grant of £40,000 to facilitate the work with the platforms extended and the new metal ends fitted. The seating plan showed seats for 90, with downstairs ones facing the centre to encourage the passengers to use the rear-half seats first. Following damage to Blundell Street depot roof in a storm, rumours came that the building may be demolished, when the preservation order failed. In contrast, the arrival of restored Bolton 66 on June 24th showed its restoration at Kearsley Power Station by a team of volunteers, led by Derek Shepherd. Undoubtedly it began the return of visiting historic cars to the Blackpool system again. Its height made 66 taller than Blackpool double-deckers, and different with Brill 21E maximum traction bogies. On its first trial run 66 derailed at Little Bispham, and so it was initially banned from turning loops. On 23rd August it was memorable for all its supporters to ride on 66 to Fleetwood, providing a contrast to the Balloons and 761 throughout the journey. In the Autumn Bolton 66 along with Dreadnought 59, did tours of the Illuminations, thus providing ideal viewing. This year concluded with a heavy snowstorm on 14th December, and there was no service until three joined Balloons with snow -plough on 722 charged the drifts. The track to Bispham was cleared on Monday but not until 19th December when trams reached Fleetwood. On the south end, OMO 7 was stranded at Harrowside for three days, with service-cars turning at Pleasure Beach.

(Left) An imposing view of 66 seen crossing Rossall fields. (Right) 66 returning to the depot after a tour in August 1981. (Author)

(Left) 762 seen on Central Promenade with the Tower in 1982. (Right) A fitter examining the bogies of 762 on the curve of Little Bispham loop during its trial-trip in 1982. (Author)

To conclude the year, 762 was nearly complete and Brush electrical equipment installed. In contrast, trailers 689 & 690 were sold to GEC Traction Company to be used for trial of their new electrical equipment at Kearsley Power Station, Bolton.

Development of new cars was shown to me by General Manager Derek Hyde, in the form of Leyland drawings showing the off-set centre exits. He said that January 1982 was the target-date of the tenders for the prototype tram, and tenders were expected from Metro-Cammel, East Lancs, Duple and Leyland. Mr. Hyde said that the control equipment could be mounted on the roof, with a tower on the top, which would be like the Coronations. The dimensions of the car would be 49 foot long and 8 ft. 2.5 ins wide , but the old E.E. wheel-sets and motors would be used in the interests of standards in the fleet. Jubilee car 762 moved under power for the first time on 31 March 1982, from the Fitting Shop into Blundell Street for the presentations to Messrs Pillar and Dyson towards their retirement. The first day on the Promenade for 762 was 1st April and subsequently during the month it was on trial and its stopping-distance measured between Bispham and Little Bispham. I was there with my camera and recorded its unpainted condition without the lower panels, so that the new bogies could be observed. Undoubtedly the bogies were much longer at 5ft 6ins, and they had self-adjusting brake mechanisms on the ends. I remember listening to the sound of the bogies, and certainly the wheel-beat was more even. Undoubtedly 762 with this new equipment was very reliable in service, but more problems had been encountered with 761. With regard of the tender for the new tram, East Lancs got the contract of £59,000 for the body and Brush got a contract of £27,000 for the electrical equipment. Track relaying was taking place in Lord Street, Fleetwood, and was hoped to be completed by Easter 1983. The finale of Blundell Street depot in October 1982 saw the scrapping of trailer 688 and Balloon 705, while all the overhead equipment was transferred to a new compound in the main depot. Demolition started in November and undoubtedly it was felt that the historic building should have been preserved as a future tramway museum.

In June 1984, the new striking Eighties livery seen on Balloon 701 and Brush-car 637 at the Casino. (Author)

PRELUDE TO THE CENTENARY WITH 641

At Easter 1983, I heard that Dreadnought was out of service because one of its motors had gone for rewinding, but on the more positive side the bogies of the new tram were to be seen in the depot looking larger than the conventional ones. Regarding the forthcoming Centenary in 1985, I was told that Derek Shepherd was forming a working team in Bolton in order to restore Conduit-car 4, Hill of Howth 10 and Pantograph 167. Traffic Manager Anthony Depledge said that the prospect of getting Edinburgh 35 looked promising, since its National Savings sponsor was prepared to cover the cost of transport here. Sheffield 513 at Beamish was also being considered for the Centenary, in exchange for Works-car 754, which they would restore as Marton Box-car 31. Incidentally 754 went out on 8th April 1983 to rescue OMO 5, which had broken its pantograph at Norbreck, and remained in reserve until 17th July 1984 when it left for Beamish. News of trams coming here for the Centenary continued and I heard that the T.M.S. had offered Glasgow Cunarder 1297 and Blackpool Standard 40. At this time it was pleasing that Coronation 660 was being repanelled in the Body Shop, and to be repainted in the original livery enhanced with chrome beading. In the Eighties a new style of green and cream livery was adopted for the Balloons, complete with a narrow band above the saloon, and wider band right round the lower panels. After a suggestion from myself 722 had "V"s painted on each end, but this was not adopted generally. On 5th June in that year, a circular tour was held by the F.T.S., using Ribble Leyland Lion bus to Knott End via Poulton, a ferry to Fleetwood and Bolton 66 for our return to Blackpool North Pier. Blackpool Transport continued this tour on the first Sunday in the month until September.

On 31st August I had a meeting with General Manager Derek Hyde, when he told me regarding the new tram that work had been delayed by the making of the body frame, which would have window frames like Atlantean buses, and upon the roof would be advertising boxes on which would be the pantograph-tower. The total cost of the prototype tram would be £138,000, against another quote of £330,000! The plans were

In 1984 a delightful scene of Edinburgh 35 unloading passengers at Gynn Square with Balloon 711 passing.

to operate the new car in 1984 for a year, and to be followed by three more each year 1985-6-7, making a total of ten to replaced the OMOs. At the same time I was pleased to hear that accident-damaged 706 was to be restored to its original open-top condition in 1985. A talk to the F.T.S. by Bernard Browne - new Chief Engineer - explained the plans for the new tram, which would be numbered 641. It would be more stylish in appearance in cream with two shades of green-lining, with "chopper" control equipment in the saloon, where it provided access for maintenance. Bogies were in the Fitting Shop complete with motors, and delivery was hoped to be early in 1984, in the event 641 arrived on 17th April 1984. On 19th November 1983, Edinburgh 35 arrived from its Shrubhill Works where it was built in 1948, and was last run on 21st October 1956. In the later period of the year, track-relaying started again on the south-bound track in Lord Street Fleetwood , between the end of October and Christmas. Edinburgh 35 moved under power from the depot to the Fitting Shop, where the track-brakes were disconnected. Works-car 754 had its trolley and the elevating-tower removed, ready for its departure to Beamish in 1984.

1984 began with Fleetwood street track completed in February, and Edinburgh 35 was repainted in its traditional livery, but unfortunately skidded in the depot and hit the Diamond "T" towing vehicle. While 706 was to be rebuilt as an open topper soon, the

Glasgow Cunarder 1297 seen with Pharos lighthouse, in an unusual setting of 1984.

A striking view of Centenary 641 returning to the depot after its first trial-run on 8th June 1984. (Right) A contrasting view of Coronation 660 seen in North Albert Street, Fleetwood. (Author)

original prototype OMO, Brush-car 638 was broken-up on 10th March. Glasgow 1297 arrived on 6th April, having travelled with police escort. Fitted with a pantograph, it went to Fleetwood where it missed the overhead on the curves round to the Ferry, and had to be towed back. Interestingly it had been exchanged for Balloon 710, which went to NTM Crich on 2nd April. On Saturday in that week, Dreadnought 59 played a part in television Les Dawson Show, on which he appeared on the top deck. On 12th April there was a great tram race between 1297 and 35, to meet at North Pier, and since 35 arrived first it won the haggis! However, the most exciting event was the arrival of new 641, and I went to East Lancs works at Blackburn to see it for the first time.

My first impression was that it was long, wide and flat-roofed, but display panels advertised the Tramway Centenary in 1985, and that East Lancs had contributed to the event. When it set off with police escorts, I followed and filmed it in various locations, including the M6 and M55. On the way it was taken to Whitbread's Brewery where it was weighed, and proved to be 10.5 tons, without its bogies. Entering Blackpool it followed the former tram route on Lytham Road, and showed TOWER on its indicator, to the surprise of the bus passengers. 641 arrived at the depot to a large crowd of workmen from the depot, garage and works, and at 4 p.m. the jacks were in place to lift it off the low-loader and lower it on to its bogies. Unfortunately, it was seen that rubbing-plates were in the wrong position, and it was left there until East Lancs workmen arrived on Monday. Its first trip on the Promenade was on 6th June, and it did create the attention of the public as totally different to all of the other trams. On Good Friday 1984, Edinburgh 35 did a special trip for Lothian employees, and subsequently went into service when I experienced it for the first time. Early in May 706 went into the Body-shop, the damaged end was rebuilt and roof removed. The sides were built up to the seat-tops level and small screens were added at the front, together with a gantry to carry the pantograph. Subsequently a short roof was made, to protect passengers from being caught by dirt. In October 1984, Sheffield 513 arrived from Beamish, unfortunately with its front dome dinted by trees en-route. At the time, I heard that another new Centenary-car would be delivered soon. 651 while looking the same as 641, would have different G.E.C. equipment and Maley &Taunton bogies from a Coronation. At this time, I organised a tour on 641 and 660, in order for us to compare their riding qualities, which was difficult! The year ended on 29th December by a tour with Sheffield 513, which reminded me of riding it in its city until 1960. Some of us got a chance to drive it, and I was warned by Beamish staff not to go too fast - as a four-wheeler could bounce off the track!

THE CENTENARY YEAR 1985

Undoubtedly this was the most memorable year from the events which were held and the variety of trams visiting Blackpool. However, in February Boat 603 left for San Fransisco, unfortunately without its proper wooden seats which were used on 706, whose top-deck seats were sent instead. Leyland bus 503 had been painted in red-and-white livery with BLACKPOOL TRAMWAY CENTENARY 1885 – 1985 on its upper panels. On Monday 22nd April 651 arrived for trial of its G.E.C. equipment, despite the loss of contract to the Brush Company for 641's equipment. Boat car 607 left for Crich in exchange for Pantograph 167, which arrived on 7th May, following Standard 40 which had arrived on 26th April. Open-top 706 was ready for a tour on the F.T.S. weekend early in May, and ran between Little Bispham and Starr Gate, which gave many of us the experience of an original open-top Balloon. Another unusual tour followed by 765 and 167, following the presentation of the Manchester "California" 765 by the M.T.M.S., who operated it at Heaton Park. The sight of these two trams travelling to Fleetwood provided a great contrast in colour and style, and enabled us to enjoy different riding experiences. The official opening of the Centenary Year was performed by Les Dawson, who was filmed on 59 reminiscent about Blackpool tram-riding during his holidays. A siding was laid at North Pier, so that each day one of the vintage trams could be on display for the public to inspect. It came into special use on 6th June when 706 was parked there, ready to be named by Princess Alice. I first saw her arrive at Starr Gate by a limousine, where she transferred to the waiting Standard 40 which took her to North Pier. Here she walked through the crowd and unveiled her name painted on the centre panel of 706. She was then presented with the souvenir Centenary plate and my "Centenary of Trams" book. She then boarded 641 to be taken to the Tower for her first trip to the top. Of course 706 is still has a new "Princess Alice" name-plate today.

A striking line-up of 1297, Railcoach 680, and open-top 706, newly-restored to its original 1934 appearance, albeit with a pantograph. (Author)

On Sunday 16th June the Open Day at the Depot & Works was held, enabling the public to visit and see the display of historic trams on the depot-fan, along with visiting all the buildings where displays of skills took place. Undoubtedly the most interesting visiting tram was 1885 Conduit-car 4, which had been restored to its original appearance without the trolley, thus being battery-powered. It was driven to North Pier for its hand-over, and returned along Princess Street on its original 1885 route to the depot. The first TRAM SUNDAY at Fleetwood took place on 14th July, with commercial vehicles on display along the streets and a shuttle-service of historic trams between Ferry and Ash Street. Hence it became an annual attraction, which continued until 2000, after which the trams were removed from the streets owing to the huge crowds. Historic trams have continued to operate a shuttle-service between North Pier and Fleetwood Tram Sunday. Also it is worth commemorating a delightful floral tram display outside St. John's Church for the Anniversary in 1985. On 30th August - Illuminations switch-on day – Hill of Howth 10 appeared on the siding at North Pier, and was received from T.M.S. President Geof Hyde by famous actress Joanna Lumley, who later switched-on the Lights. On the day before the Centenary Day I organised a tour on Howth 10, which provided a unique way of seeing all the historic trams operating on that day. Its high railings round the upper deck enabled you to stand and photograph passing trams easily.

(Above left) Conduit 4 after the Centenary procession in 1985. (Right) Manchester 765 on tour at Fleetwood as a POST CAR. (Below) Pantograph 167 and 765 at Fleetwood Ferry on 11th May 1985. (Author)

(Above left) 59 in the Centenary procession, followed by another eighteen trams. (Below left) John Bull arrives at Pleasure Beach. (Right) Boat 606 15th in procession, turning on to the loop, followed by 1297, 8, 513, 726 & 66. (Author)

Sunday 29th September was blessed with a fine and sunny day, and thousands of people came to see the historic tram procession at Blackpool. All those with a ticket had to board their allocated tram at the depot. Twenty trams left in order, with some reversing at Bispham and some at Cabin, then returning to North Pier where leading trams: 4, 59, 40, 167 & 706, waited. The last to leave the depot for North Pier were Dreadnought 59 and 4, which stood on the centre track there, surrounded by the crowds who watched the arrival of the official party by landaus, dressed in Victorian costumes. After the official photographs, the crowd were astonished at the arrival of the unexpected steam tram engine "John Bull" of 1885. Watching the procession from the tower-wagon on Central Promenade, enabled me to see the finest sight ever seen on the tramway, visiting trams being dispersed among the familiar ones from Blackpool. As the procession passed, the climax came with "John Bull" whistling and blowing steam as the 20th member of the procession. At Pleasure Beach, the procession was lined-up, with historic ones on the outer loop. John Bull reversed at Harrowside and returned to the depot as did Conduit 4, while the other trams carried passengers all day. Sheffield 513 went to Princess Street to form the subject of the Tram-Pull Competition, which was won by the Blackpool Transport team! However the Last Night of the Proms formed the finale of the Centenary, when a tour of the Illuminations by historic trams was followed by a hot-pot supper served from Coronation 660 on Pleasure Beach loop. There was a firework display and sing-song at North Pier, when we could return to the depot by a historic tram of our choice. In December there was a final tour on Conduit 4, which traversed the historic track to Foxhall with Victorian-dressed passengers, and then with Standard 40 went to Starr Gate and Tower for the final time.

PROLOGUE OF TONY DEPLEDGE
1977 TO 2001

Tony Depledge first started with Blackpool Transport in Janua 1969 as both conductor and driver. Following his Universi degree, he worked on transport in both Midlands and Sou Yorkshire, and then in 1977 he returned to Blackpool Transpo as Traffic Manager. He certainly found it a prestigious firr and learned a lot from Derek Hyde, whose experience ha always been with Municipal Authorities. Recalling the arriv of Bolton 66 in 1981, Tony commends the good quality of i restoration and having a clear agreement that 66 was part c the operating fleet. Undoubtedly the Centenary in 1985 was triumph for the co-operation of all members of the Transpc Department staff, as stewards of the historic tramway. 1986, Tony became the Managing Director of Blackpo Transport Services, when the financial situation change and the Council's subsidy was lost, although they retaine the maintenance of their tramway. While many events c his years as Managing Director are recorded in this chapte Tony Depledge is especially pleased to have succeeded recovering Standard 147 from Trolleyville U.S.A., as a goo addition to the fleet. This was strengthened by his team – Mik Airey, Chris Pulling, Graham Twidale – who worked on its retur to Blackpool. Today Tony is a Director of Transport Policy i Arriva PLC, but he looks back with pleasure on his 24 yea at Blackpool Transport. Certainly, as an author I have alwa found him charming and helpful, and he is seen here with m in front of 700 with one of my new books in 1997.

Tony Depledge being presented with copies of "By Tram To The Tower" by Steve Palmer in front of restored 700. (Gazette)

THE NEW BLACKPOOL TRANSPORT SERVICES

Managing Director - Tony Depledge 1986 -2001

The Company came into being on 20th October, and took over operation on Sunday 26th October, by this time the trams and buses were wearing a vinyl showing a new Company logo, replacing the Municipal coat-of-arms. Incidentally the Board of Directors comprised principal management and Councillors of Blackpool Borough Council. It was interesting that in 1986 the next batch of Centenary cars 642-644 were delivered in November, when the new bogies were waiting for them in the depot. A further three cars 645-647 were on order for delivery in April 1987, and they would be financed by BTS shares for the Corporation. Tony Depledge told me that G.E.C. car 651's body would be bought and re-equipped with the same bogies and Brush "Chopper" equipment as the others. That would make a total of eight Centenary cars and with Jubilee cars 761 & 762 would provide ten for winter service. I was disappointed to gather that we would not see a further three Centenary cars 648-650, which would have completed the class, and deduced that funds were now limited. The seating arrangement would be more like 651 than 641, along with the tower and lack of advertising panels. At the time it was declared that advertising boxes could be made by B.T.S., but this never happened.

As the new Centenary cars came into service, the OMOs were withdrawn, and in 1986 I learned that the next would be 3, 6 and 7, which had the highest mileage of 160,000. However there was a future for 7, because its under-frame and running equipment would be used to create a B & F Vanguard crossbench-car number 619. Regarding the maintenance of the overhead-line, its costs were now charged to the Borough, while running-repairs to the trams were carried by B.T.S., reflecting the ownership of the tramway. Thus the tramway track, overhead and depot were owned by the Corporation, while the trams were owned by B.T.S.. In Christmas 1986 trams were running to Starr Gate again, when the track and point-work at Pleasure Beach had been relaid, together with a new crossover between the points of the loop. This replaced the old crossover at Dean Street, and enabled quick-reversal when the loop was closed during the winter. At the same time the three new Centenary cars 642-644 were seen in the depot, but they had not run under power yet, until Brush had come to commission them in January 1987. It was interesting for me to find out that the overhead-line was now lasting for 17 years as against 10 years in the past, thanks to the new pantographs. Before the end of the year we had Coronation 660 for a festive tour, and were sorry to see that the Corporation badges had been removed, including those in the saloon. This left a gap in the driver's-door, which was always a ventilator concealed by a plaque with the coat-of-arms. However we were pleased to see that OMO 11 was the only tram left with the Municipal badges.

On February 24th 1987, 643 entered service and OMO 3 was dragged on to "the land" next to the remains of OMO 2 there. Of the remaining OMOs, 1, 5, 8 ,11 were in green and cream, while 6, 7, 9, 12 were still in red, and looking decidedly scruffy. OMO 7 was withdrawn in February and left on 16th March for the workshop at Mode Wheel in Salford Docks where Brush car 290 was being rebuilt by Keith Terry for the N.T.M. at Crich. At Easter I remember that Good Friday had a poor service, with Atlantean buses being used to Cleveleys, having been seen at the tram station there. The prototype Balloon 700 was still in the Seventies livery and was extensively rebuilt in July, being repainted in the better style, and also the Western Train was being refurbished. On 4th July a memorable tour was held, being called "Totally Topless Tour" and thus using Howth 10, Dreadnought 59 and Balloon 706. Being an ideal sunny day, it was a most enjoyable tour of the whole system, enabling us to capture these trams together in a variety of locations including Fleetwood street-track. Vanguard 619 arrived on 29th July, but two days later the Railway Inspector failed it for service until it was fitted with full-width lifeguards and better lights. Work on 619 continued by the volunteers at Blackpool, making the wooden crossbench seats and fitting them. Centenaries 645 and 646 were expected in August, and the new bogies were awaiting them in the depot. After intensive work on 619, the Railway Inspector saw it again on 27th August, and it had to have the lattice platform gates altered, with access from the saloon. However it went into service during the Illuminations, and certainly the public enjoyed riding on it. My only reservation was the pantograph which looked unsuitable, as opposed to a traditional trolley on such a car.

New Centenary 647 looking imposing for the traditional tram route in Lord Street, Fleetwood 1988. (Author)

Howth 10 and Dreadnought 59, two topless trams on the tour, reversing at Ash Street, Fleetwood. (Author)

In conversation with Tony Depledge on 29th October 1987, he enlightened me on the present B.T.S. situation. He said the finances of the new Company were satisfactory and they would be declared in March 1988, and so were to be expected to break-even. Incidentally, £25,000 was paid to the Council as a nominal "rental" by B.T.S.. However the Blackpool Council budget for the permanent-way was £650,000 per annum, of which 65% was paid by Lancashire County Council, leaving Blackpool to find £227,500. Regarding the Glasgow Garden Festival next year, Blackpool had not offered Boat 607 which had been at Crich, and probably one of the others 606 would be renovated. Also the matter of bringing B & F Box 40 here for the 90th anniversary of the Tramroad in 1988, Tony said he was in favour of that, providing that the work could be finished. Of course restoration work on 40 had been undertaken at Heaton Park in Manchester, with new side panels being fitted, re-wiring taking place, and finally by April its bogies were fitted with new tyres by British Rail at Derby. A sponsor was to be found, who would be interested in paying £4,000 a year for two years, with an option on a third year. In fact the well-known local manufacturer "Fisherman's Friend" did this, and thus 40 came in 1988 advertising their products. During the winter in 1987, works were done on the system, including light-weight overhead at Starr Gate loop, resulting in single-line working from Harrowside for the service-cars. During track work at Gynn Square thus fitting of new points, single-line working was operated from Cabin to North Pier, and unfortunately Works Brush car 659 pushed its trailer 260 into the workings, but it was retrieved for further use in transporting track.

Vanguard 619 at Starr Gate during the first tour on 31st October 1987, but sadly its tower and pantograph look inappropriate for such a vintage tram. (Author)

Box 40 in the appropriate location of Fleetwood during Tram Sunday 1989, with crowds and vintage buses. (Author)

1988 - 90TH ANNIVERSARY OF
BLACKPOOL & FLEETWOOD TRAMWAY

In 1988 the finally-produced Centenary 647 went into service on 30th April, while OMO 6 & 9 were broken-up in the yard. Balloon 724 was repainted in a so-called new livery, in fact reverting to the Sixties style, and so I suggested that the green paint round the saloon windows was swept-down and under the windscreens, thus dividing the all-cream front. This was done to 724 in March, and it was subsequently followed to all repainted Balloons, making a better appearance. For the Season the Fleetwood service was a 12-minute frequency, operated alternately by Centenary OPOs and railcoaches, but double-deckers appeared only on Market Days as "specials". It was a great satisfaction to me when Box 40 arrived from Heaton Park on Tuesday 14th June, twenty-five years since it was last here. Although it "burnt-out" one of its motors on its first run to North Pier, the motor was re-wound and thus enabled 40 to lead the procession to Fleetwood Tram Sunday. By this time the advertisement-boards had been fitted between the bogies, which were not ideal in appearance. Its Corporation indicator boxes at each end were also fitted during the first week in August, and plaques were fitted above the saloon doors recording its preservation. Thus its appearance on this tramway commemorated the 90th Anniversary of the Blackpool & Fleetwood Tramroad, and certainly was an ideal sight.

Elsewhere, events were worth recording, since the Glasgow Garden Festival would have a working tramway, and Blackpool sent Boat 606 painted in a blue-and-yellow livery advertising Bellhaven Beers on 2nd March 1988. A few days later Edinburgh 35 was sent to Glasgow, along with Cunarder 1297 and Paisley 68 from Crich. I remember visiting the Garden Festival with a party from Crich, before it opened to the public. It was appropriate that the President that year was Derek Shepherd, undoubtedly a great restorer of historic trams for Blackpool in 1985. Undoubtedly it was quite a novelty to ride along the Clyde again, this time in the Govan area. Of course I filmed the trams there, and it was very appropriate to see the famous paddle-steamer Waverley passing at the same time. On the same occasion we called to see the new Summerlee Transport Museum near Glasgow, albeit with a Brussels car operating.

At the present it is pleasing that Glasgow Coronation 1245 has returned there, having been seen at Carlton Colville and even visited Blackpool depot. Undoubtedly it will be nice to ride on a Coronation in the Glasgow area once again! At Beamish in County Durham on 7th August 1988, Marton open-top 31 made its inaugural-run, having been restored to its original condition in the red-and-white livery. It was a great achievement, considering that it arrived there in the works-car condition of 754. In due course 31 returned to Blackpool for the Tramroad Centenary Anniversary in 1998 and again in 2010 for the 125th Anniversary of the Promende Tramway.

Undoubtedly the attraction of historic trams on the Blackpool system was manifested on Sunday April 9th 1989 when the film "A Man from the Prudential" was filmed in North Albert Street, Fleetwood. This was dated 1931 in Liverpool, and therefore the two cars Bolton 66 and Howth 10 were disguised as cars from that city. Since Howth 10 was due to return to Crich in that year, a tour was held on 21st October for the final time, and undoubtedly we enjoyed the experience of riding on this distinctive tram, especially with its high upper-deck railings and it outward-facing seats along the saloon. While it was re-gauged for its operation here in 1985, sadly it has never since operated at the National Tramway Museum. In more conventional events for the Blackpool tram fleet, 761 & 762 were repainted in a new-style Atlantean livery, with green window-frames, roof and lower skirt. In February 1989, Box 40 had its seats removed by a team of volunteers, which were taken to Salford Mode Wheel workshop, where they were re-covered with tartan-pattern moquette, formerly used on the Swift buses which were withdrawn in 1987. In August 1989, Brush-car 636 was repainted in the wartime green livery, and a tour was held driven by Philip Higgs dressed in a metal-helmet and carrying a gas-mask. In this year Sheffield 513 returned to Beamish, since they had acquired another Sheffield car Standard 264.

Glasgow Garden Festival 1988 with native Cunarder 1297 and Boat 606 in blue-and-yellow livery. Ironic that 606 is now in U.S.A. in exchange for Standard 147. (Author)

(Left) Overhead-line works-car 754 on 8th April 1983, its last working day in Blackpool. (Right) As restored to its original appearance as 31 by Beamish Open Air Museum in 1988. (R.P.Fergusson)

NEW DEVELOPMENTS IN 1990

At the beginning of 1990, 648 went into service re-equipped with the Brush "Chopper" equipment. At the same time, Centenary 641 was overhauled and fitted with new window-frames, since the original ones had rusted, and also its wheels were re-tyred. Also interesting was the rebuilding of Balloon 701, which was fitted with safety-glass and the front curved glass removed. For the first time the swing-over seats were replaced by the bus-seats, which were fixed facing forward in each half of the tram's saloon. 701 was ultimately repainted in the red-and-white livery of the Blackpool Routemasters, when complete. When it first ran to North Pier on 17th February 1991, in my view this looked very attractive and would have been a good new livery for the tram fleet, but this did not happen. 701 was also fitted with a pantograph. Some Boats were repainted at the time, including 604 in the same red-and-white livery. On the other hand, 602 was painted in the yellow-and-black Handy-bus livery, which is still today. Also the Boats - apart from 600 at Heaton Park - were fitted with new twin-windscreens. It is clear that by this time such changes were improvements for the trams, and the main service was operated by the Centenaries and still some OMOs.

At a visit to Tony Depledge on 4th January 1990, I heard the most exciting news that Czech TATRA KT8 D5 may come in June on trial for the Season. This was said to be a two-section articulated car and 2.5 metres wide, however in retrospect it did not appear, since there was some concern about its power for the sub-stations here. Regarding the historic-cars visiting, there was some suggestion that Sheffield 513 may return again, and there was also a suggestion that Liverpool "Baby Grand" 245 might come here. Chief Engineer Bill Gibson went to inspect it, but it was found not to be in condition to operate, since it had last run on September 14th 1957. At the time, it also was suggested that Blackpool open-topper 31 should return in the future, and it did happen at the end of 1997, for the Centenary in the following year. Regarding Coronation 304, which still had the original "Vambac" equipment and was at St.Helens Transport Museum for restoration, Tony Depledge was unenthusiastic about its return here. His experience as a driver of these Coronations once resulted from the failing of the electric-brakes at Ash Street, and the likely collision with a lorry crossing the tram lines in front, which fortunately moved out of the Coronation's way at the last minute!

Brush-car 636 in wartime livery with 762 in North Albert Street, Fleetwood, near to the Market. (Author)

A new livery for the twin-cars was taking place on 671-681, with a green roof and a green skirt, but unfortunately all-green doors. Boat car 605 was being overhauled at the time, being fitted with E.E. Z-4 controllers and painted in the original livery with the F.T.S. badge on the side, as its sponsor. Centenary 641 was repainted in a new-style livery already seen on 646, and like the twin-cars. In May 1990 I remember organising a tour on Box 40 and Dreadnought 59, and on a sunny day they made a contrasting sight.

(Left) The striking livery of 701 at Pleasure Beach in 1991.

(Right) In depot 700 & 762 in different liveries. (Author)

Dreadnought 59 and Box 40 in contrasting liveries and style, on Central Promenade in a final tour together in May 1990. (Author)

This was the last year for 59 to be in Blackpool after thirteen years, and a final tour was held on 11th November before it returned to N.T.M. at Crich. Unfortunately, after a short display in the exhibition hall, 59 was removed to the store at Clay Cross, and has never been seen by the public again. On a more positive note here, track-relaying was taking place at Fleetwood North Albert Street and subsequently the Ferry loop. In other places tramway development was now taking place: Manchester was preparing for its new light-rail system in the city-centre by laying track in High Street, Mosely Street and Aytoun Street, and work was to start in Piccadilly in January 1991. Also approval had been given for the Sheffield super-tram system by the Government, with a £50 million grant, and it was planned for starting in 1993. Certainly this was very encouraging for the future, considering that Blackpool had been the only U.K. tramway operator, since the closing of the Glasgow City tram-system in 1962. In fact trams returned to Manchester on 4th April 1992, when the first one ran from Bury to Victoria Station. On April 27th the first tram ran through the city centre and appropriately its number was 1007, the same as the last tram in January 1949 which left Piccadilly for Birchfields Road depot. Thus history was almost being repeated - in a positive way.

THE ARRIVAL OF BOX 40 & STOCKPORT 5 & THE FASCINATING RESTORATION OF 700

In January 1996 I was pleased to learn that it was arranged with Crich that Box 40 would return to Blackpool this year. To facilitate this, money was raised for the cost of transportation and repainting 40, by a group of enthusiasts "Friends of 40"and Fleetwood Tram Sunday Committee. A Centenary Committee was started by B.T.S., at which it was announced that Beamish agreed to allow open-top 31 to come here for twelve months, with the provision that it could be repainted. Box 40 returned to its native system on April 22nd, and I was pleased to see it travelling at speed on the M55. At the depot, headlights were fitted beneath the front dash, and also the indicator boxes brought back. On the 8th May, 40 was given trial-run along the Promenade, and in June came to Fleetwood for a presentation of 40 to Michael Morton of B.T.S. by Jim Cowpe of Tram Sunday Committee, and were given a return ride to Ash Street. Shortly after this, 40 went into the Paint Shop, where it was rubbed-down and painted, and the gold-leaf lettering was used on "BLACKPOOL & FLEETWOOD ELECTRIC TRAMROAD". On the head-boards, Fleetwood Tram Sunday and the North Euston Hotel were credited. There was a feeling at B.T.S. that it would be appropriate if air-brakes were fitted to 40 for safety on the Promenade, but the T.M.S. owners wanted it to retain its original-style. However, another historic car was added to the fleet, when Stockport 5 was handed-over in June by its owner Stan Heaton, having been restored at the Mode Wheel workshops in Salford. Thus Tram Sunday was quite exciting when the tram procession was led by Box 40, followed by Stockport 5 and the new Walls Ice Cream Tram 719. The latter Balloon was a great novelty, passengers being able to board, buy and eat ice-cream on the tram, while watching the transport vehicles on display. While the working team from Mode Wheel was given a ride on Stockport 5 to Fleetwood Ferry, it was then returned to the depot to be fitted with air-brakes for safety.

Stockport 5 on it first tour 17th May 1998 at Thornton Gate, stopped for the photographers. (Author)

700 looking very striking in its restored appearance and livery at Cabin on 28th March 1997. (Author)

In the same year there was a discussion with B.T.S that the inaugural open-topper 700 of 1934 should be restored to its rebuilt wartime condition as an enclosed Balloon. Therefore this would be painted in the wartime mainly green-livery decorated by cream flares, together with the Municipal coat-of-arms. Also it would have the material-covered hard seats on the upper-deck, which had originally been all-wooden, and the ceilings would resemble the original alhambrinal. Also it was intended to have the half-drop windows using the modern shatter-glass, also having modern curved windows made by Pilkingtons in the same shape. Looking at the outside appearance, it was intended to install new opening windscreens in stainless-steel, and a row of imitation ventilators above the lower saloon windows. During August 1996, work began with the stripping of the body down to the body-frame, and strengthening the under-frame. Once 700 was in the Body Shop, Mike Airey found he had to change some of the plans, in that the hard-seats from 702 would not be suitable now, and the making of new front curved-windows would be too expensive, and so the plate-glass ones were retained. However the plans to return to the original twin-indicators were made, and also mock side-indicators only to show PROMENADE. I observed its restoration, and listened to Mike Airey about its progress. He told me that it had been decided to restore the silver-appearance of the E.E. Z6 controllers, to be scrubbed by a firm at Sheffield. Inside the saloons, it was intended to simulate the original linoleum, in colours of a brown passage and green under the seats. The woodwork was restored to its original colour, wooden strips were fitted to the ceiling, and green panels under the windows. In a point of detail, shiny-metal numbers 237 were fitted above the doors, and stainless-steel strips were restored to the fenders. 700 was painted during November, but the only error was in the windscreens, which arrived as four right-hand ones, of which only two could be fitted. Eventually new left-hand ones were also made in Glasgow.

Crossbench 2 and Pantograph 167 at Crich on their inaugural day before leaving for Blackpool on 22 June.

THE CENTENARY OF BLACKPOOL & FLEETWOOD TRAMWAY 1998

Undoubtedly this was a memorable year, commencing with notable trams and special events. Fundamentally it commenced with a tour on 40 and the arrival of both Marton open-top 31 and articulated-car Trampower 611. We gathered that it was here to be on test, having come from Birkenhead where it used the Pacific Road line. Also Balloon 707 was the first to be rebuilt with flat-ends, but looking quite smart in a new-style green and cream livery. Boat 600 had returned from Heaton Park, and was fitted with its trolley-tower and painted in the traditional livery. By the end of January the track through Cleveleys Square was being relaid, with a single-line service to Little Bispham. In early February SPENO unit was here, eliminating the corrugations between Cocker Street and Gynn Square, Metropole street-track, South Shore and Fleetwood street-track At the end of March a surprising visitor was Glasgow Coronation 1245, which came from EATM in Carlton Colville, for storage here and evaluation of its future role. Also by this time the depot contained two Balloons 700 and 703 which were in the wartime livery, and provided the sight of the Forties and Fifties cars seen again. In April, articulated 611 was first seen on the Promenade being towed by 754, and was subsequently seen under power. At the beginning of May, the F.T.S. weekend featured a tour of the system using Boat 600 and Princess Alice 706, both giving open-air rides. A tour on Stockport 5 was held on May 17th for its supporters, which was a sunny day and provided the experience of riding on an open-top 4-wheeler over the light-rail track to Fleetwood. Occasionally it lost its trolley, which had to be grasped by one of the top-deck passengers, but the sight of this red-and-white open-topper on Fleetwood streets attracted the attention of the local residents. However they would have missed the early morning trial-run to Fleetwood by 611 at 0533 from Manchester Square, before the service-car. It seemed to run well, but being low-loading was near to the ground and gave the pantograph a long reach to the overhead.

Here Crossbench 2 and Pantograph 167 are seen at the depot, about to unload on to the rail.

Depot open-day on 28th June 1998, seen with 5, 660 and 167. (Author)

Meanwhile at Crich work was being completed on B & F crossbench car 2, which had been reconstructed with a new under-frame and was repainted, together with Pantograph 167 which was painted in its attractive green livery. They were both in operation on 21st June 1998, together with Toastrack 166, which provided an attractive sight and good riding experience. Incidentally, the trial of historic track in Princess Street and Blundell Street, and its crossing from the Promenade at Foxhall Square was used by 754 and Centenary 645 on June 9th, ready for its use on the depot open-day. Certainly it was good to see trams in this location once again. On Sunday 22nd June, 2 and 167 arrived in Blackpool, travelling along the Promenade on low-loaders to Manchester Square. Unfortunately they were first taken into the bus yard, and had to be moved on to the approach-track behind the Works. It was interesting to first see Pantograph 167 rolled-off the loader and pulled into the depot, followed by its trolley-tower on a barrow. Since 2 was still fitted with its trolley, it rolled on to the rails, the trolley was raised to the overhead and was driven towards the depot. Before entering, it fused the substation, depriving the power from the depot, and therefore had to be pushed in. Perhaps it had been wrongly re-wired? On 24th June, albeit on a rainy day, 167 and 2 were to be seen going to Fleetwood, in order to give B.T.S. drivers some experience. The sight of each of these cars provided me with the memory of Pantograph cars in service on the route, and 2 as Engineering-car 127. Open Day at the depot was held on Sunday 28th June, and there was a line-up of historic trams on the depot track-fan, including 2, 40, 31, 167 and

Boat 607 on Princess Street curve with it trolley being held on, and 31 being watched as it is partly derailed and then withdrawn. (Author)

Coronation 660. A shuttle-service was run from North Pier via Princess Street and Blundell Street, using 31 and Boats 600 and 607. Unfortunately, the old junction to the former depot derailed 31 twice, and it had to be changed for Bolton 66, but it was quite an experience to travel this way on a tram. At the end of the afternoon, Michael Morton decided to send twin-car 675-685 on the circular via Foxhall, and it had to be watched for derailing on several locations. However the Open-Day included displays of historic buses, model layouts and stalls in the bus garage, and visitors were able to tour the workshops, which were usually never seen by the public.

On 1st July it was a fine and sunny day to commemorate the first Tramroad ride to Fleetwood on crossbench car 4 in 1898. 2 and 40 started from North Pier, carrying the official party and a television crew respectively. Beginning at Little Bispham, a crowd of schoolchildren cheered the cars when passing many of the stops on the route. The climax coming at Fleetwood Ash Street, where Chaucer Road School sent a large crowd to greet the arrival of 2 & 40. This was just as it had been a hundred years ago, as my grandmother had remembered and told me about it. The sight of Crossbench 2 amongst the traffic and travelling down the streets to the Ferry, was undoubtedly memorable. Subsequently, on Saturdays 4th and 11th July, the three heritage cars 2, 40 & 167 shuttled between Cleveleys and Fleetwood, giving free rides to all the enthusiasts from the Tramway Museum Society. The public watched them pass the stops, and would probably have liked to ride on them. The Centenary procession was held on Sunday 12th July, when unfortunately the weather was awful with howling gale and pouring rain. The trams assembled at Pleasure Beach loop and journeyed to Fleetwood headed by 2, 619, 40, 167, 31 and 600, followed by many others. Unlike the same occasion in 1985, few people turned out to watch them, but the cars were well-filled despite being open-cars and cross-bench 2. A lunch was held at the North Euston Hotel, and the T.L.R.S. held a great display of model layouts at the Marine Hall. Fortunately on 16th July the weather was fine and sunny for the tour on 2, 40 & 167, enabling us to record them in appropriate locations, including Central Promenade on their way back to the depot. This had been a last view of 2, because it was not allowed to take part in Tram Sunday on 19th July, a big disappointment to Fleetwood. Although the organisers had contributed to the cost of trams coming, this car was viewed as dangerous in the streets with crowds of people, in case any tried to jump on the running-boards and fall off. However, it was good to see and ride on Marton open-top 31 and Pantograph 167 on this occasion. The two visiting cars 2 and 167 returned to Crich on July 27-28th, but we will hope to see 167 here again in 2010!

A nostalgic scene on the historic journey of 2 to Fleetwood on 1st July 1998, cheered by the children of the local school, as it slows down at Little Bispham. (Right) 167 at Gynn Square on its return to depot, having missed its historic journey to North Station! (Author)

A fine scene of 2, 40, 167 together at Ferry on 11th July, and their final scene together in Lytham Road, upon their return to depot. Sadly, they were never seen together again. (Author)

APPROACHING THE 21ST CENTURY WITH THE RETURN OF 147

Once the events of the anniversary were over, in November 1998 the approach track to the depot was relayed, and also Boat 605 was repainted in the wartime livery, which these trams never had. News came that Standard 147 was hoping to be recovered from Trolleyville in Ohio. At a cost of £40,000 for its transport back to Blackpool. 1999 began with the customary tour on 40, but when the car emerged from Lytham Road, the sea was coming over, and we decided to travel north to Fleetwood as soon as possible. In May, Boat car 604 was repainted in the modern style with a green skirt and no traditional green flare - not appropriate. On August 7th there was a dramatic derailment of 710 at Cavendish Road stop, and it had 90 passengers. The front bogie left the rails and ploughed into the sleepers, and it seemed that the springs were missing from the chairs and thus the track was wide of gauge. The track had to be relayed with new sleepers, chairs and ballast. A meeting with Tony Depledge provided me with plans for the future, when I mentioned the Marton Tramway Centenary on May 23rd 2001, he commented on the possibility of recovering Standard 147 from the U.S.A.. There would be an offer to Trolleyville that there would be an exchange of 147 for Boat 606, which could be operated there unlike the tall 147 was unable to.

On January 7th 2000 a new crossover was completed at Broadwaters, to the north of the road- crossing thus enabling school-specials to reverse here for Cardinal Allen School. Work then started on the worn-out track on the road-crossing, which had to be closed and the trams worked single-line to Thornton Gate. This continued for eight weeks, until the Police and Wyre Borough Council complained to Blackpool, and two track-gangs worked overtime to complete the job by 17th March. Also in Fleetwood, on 18th April Brush car 630 left the track on the curve from Pharos Street to North Albert Street, and its pantograph left the overhead. It was pushed back on by the tower wagon, and ran in reverse round by the Ferry to the North Albert Street crossover. By this year, times had changed for the trams: 718 was ready to be rebuilt like 707 and 709, while OMO 5 left for N.T.M. on June 2nd but was stored in Clay Cross store with Dreadnought 59. Of the illuminated trams, Rocket and Western Train were withdrawn from use owing to their condition, but 735 Hovertram and 736 Frigate were still in service. In June 2000, the bad news of the period was the strike by the platform staff, who manned a picket-line at the depot, and prevented inspectors bringing trams out. On 16th July it was Tramless Sunday at Fleetwood, and became the end of trams running through crowds to the Ferry, which the staff claimed was unsafe.

In June 2000 discussion was taking place about the return of Standard 147 from Trolleyville U.S.A., and I was told that Tony Depledge was trying to identify the owner who bought it for £50 in 1967. Chris Pulling, one of the planners, proposed that enthusiasts should raise money towards the restoration of 147 when it returned to Blackpool. It was agreed that Boat 606 would be sent to Trolleyville in exchange for 147, and that a team would got there to prepare 147 for its return by sea. I remember 606 coming to Fleetwood with 604 and 605 on 22nd August, and I photographed its return to Pleasure Beach, possibly for the last time. It had the windscreen removed on 28th August, but it made a secret journey to Fleetwood for the U.S.A. team, and it departed for Seaforth docks on 14th September for being loaded on to the Atlantic Conveyer. Mike Airey told me that 606 arrived at Trolleyville, and operated on the same day, without its tower, but subsequently Trolleyville closed down and 606 went to the Cleveland system. On Wednesday 18th October Standard 147 returned and landed at Seaforth. Mike Airey reported on the television that when his team saw it at Trolleyville, it was filthy with racoons living inside it. They hosed it down, and dirt ran down the side of it. They separated the two decks, and it went to be loaded at Boston on 2nd October. It arrived at Rigby Road depot yard on 23rd October, the two decks were joined together again, and mounted on the bogies. It was then pushed into the depot where it looked very unsightly compared with the other trams there. I remember Tony Depledge and Bill Gibson looking somewhat surprised at its dishevelled condition, but he decided that it should be restored by Easter 2002.

Final scenes of 606 on 22nd August 2000, as it poses at Fleetwood Ferry with bus 363, and seen returning with passengers at Fisherman's Walk. (Author)

(Above) 147 in the Body Shop during its restoration as seen upon return from the U.S.A. (Left) First seen from the Works before fully complete. (Right) Valhalla, 720 & 147 in the depot compound nearly completed. (Author)

The restoration of 147 proceeded during 2001, with the bogies fitted with new 30-inch tyres obtained from Brussels. In the Body Shop the panelling was removed from the lower-deck and new teak panelling fitted, together with new dash-panels. Towards the end of 2001 its roof was covered with fibreglass rather than the traditional painted canvas, both staircases had been re-fitted with treads, painted and fixed. Since steps and brake-rods were missing, some were taken off 753, while wooden seats were rubbed-down and repainted. In the lower saloon all the woodwork was restored, and the seat-cushions re-made and covered with moquette correctly. Safety-glass was ordered for the curved panels at each end, and the frame had been welded with oxide for strength. The aim was to complete 147 by Easter 2002, but since Tony Depledge was leaving for a new appointment, 147 was pulled out of the Fitting Shop on 27th September, so that he could be presented with cheques for 147 from Friends of Forty and F.T.S.. I remember it was fully repainted, but without its numbers and lining, so I went upstairs and sat on the balcony once more, as in 1966.

(Above) 633 CEVIC in Hopton Road with 735 Hovertram on 1st August 2001. (Right) Profile of CEVIC at Fleetwood Ferry looking like a trawler.

THE FUTURE OF THE TRAMWAY IN A NEW CENTURY

Managing Director Steve Burd 2001 - 2009

Early in 2001 I learned that a new illuminated car was to be created using Brush-car 633. Since this was due to be scrapped because its under-frame was rotten, a completely new one was to be built on which the vertical pillars would support the new flat roof carrying a ship's superstructure. It was therefore to be a trawler, sponsored by Fisherman's Friend of Fleetwood, and advertising their famous products. By August it had become trawler "CEVIC" having taken the shape, with plastic tubes along the sides to ripple like water. An inverter was positioned above the centre-platform, in order to change the voltage of the lighting from 550 volts D/C to 24 volts A/C. The superstructure was all in position, and white panels of the bridge would be illuminated from inside. On 29th September 633 CEVIC sailed to Fleetwood to arrive at Fisherman's Walk by 8 p.m., and certainly it looked impressive with the high bows and its profile illuminated by red-and-white bulbs. The front-deck featured a winding-reel and a frame for raising the nets, and on the stern-deck a lifeboat. Mrs Doris Lofthouse received it on behalf of Fisherman's Friend, and pointed out that it would operate throughout the year. The saloon seated 48 passengers on fixed seats, with attractive coloured moquette, and a centre-platform with non-slip floor. CEVIC 633 did appear in service during 2001, and while it was double-ended, it hardly looked correct going stern-first. By the end of the year 147 was nearly finished, with brass handles being fitted on the platform, ticket-boxes and side-indicator boxes from former Standards - like 177.

Steve Burd seen giving a speech at the launching of restored Western Train on 14th May 2009, shortly before he left Blackpool for the Midlands. (Author)

2002 was notable in January by the relaying of the Norbreck and Little Bispham sleeper-track by Birse of Manchester. Since a single-line tram service was operated, Birse had to work from the cliff-side, and it was not easy when the overhead was live. After this, Birse insisted that for safety the overhead was switched-off, and the trams could not run alongside track-relaying. In the early months of 2002, 147's paint was completed by being gold-lined. I learned that it would be launched on Wednesday 3rd April. However I was not pleased to hear from one of the B.T.S. management that the traditional green-and-cream livery on trams was to be replaced on the trams by a design of yellow with different colours of bus routes. However, rebuilt 709 was seen having trials on the new track, and 761 was in a new green-and-cream style of livery. However on 28th March I saw the impressive sight of 147 in Cleveleys Square on its way to Fleetwood, and undoubtedly the public admired it. I followed 147 by car, and captured it in various locations, noticing that its indicators showed RESERVED and were traditionally black-and-white. A rope hung from the trolley, which still had a swivel-head. On 3rd April, 147 arrived at the Pleasure Beach loop and took its invited passengers to North Pier, where the ceremony was performed by Joan Humble M.P.. There followed a splendid ride to Fleetwood, which reminded me of a last ride on 147 in October 1966. At the Ferry I met Steve Burd for the first time, and he subsequently admitted that he was amazed at the dedicated following of Blackpool trams, as he witnessed on that occasion. The first use of 147 for passengers took place on Saturday 6th April 2002, when it first travelled along the Promenade between Cabin and Pleasure Beach. I was delighted when the Inspector sent it to Fleetwood, and I heard the distinctive sound of the wheels and watched the swaying of the body during its journey over the sleeper-track. Undoubtedly, it was perfect to capture it passing Pharos Lighthouse, through Albert Square and along Lord Street, reminding me of it running on the Marton route years ago!

(Above) On 6th April 2002, 147 making its first public journey, with Pharos Lighthouse, and at Fleetwood Ferry. (Below) 147 with Big Max at Pleasure Beach. (Author)

RETURN OF CORONATION 304 - THANKS TO SALVAGE SQUAD

Equally momentous on the Blackpool tramway was the return on 9th June 2002 of Coronation 304, which was brought back from St. Helens Transport Museum. When it arrived at the depot on a low-loader, I was surprised when I saw it was without the side panels, although it was complete at the ends with number 641 - the same as a Centenary. Apart from this, the triumph was the success by Philip Higgs of L.T.T. in responding to an appeal by Salvage Squad of Channel 4, who wanted to portray 50 year-old creations, like the Coronations. Its restoration was to take place in a fenced compound at the back of track-1 in the depot, and filmed by Salvage Squad. On 28th June I went to see it, saw the VAMBAC mounted on a stand and brake-shoes were lying in pairs on the floor. Inside the saloon the seats were missing along with the window-frames at one side. Also panels were removed from both sides of the fluorescent lights, to reveal the main cables from the controls at the front to the VAMBAC equipment over the centre-platform. Brian Pickup of N.T.M. at Crich was working in trying to re-wire 304, but I formed the impression that it proved to be a problem. However during the year, a team from Salvage Squad were filmed panelling the sides, although L.T.T. did most of it themselves. Kevin Graham - a retired electrician from the depot - was called in to help rewire the VAMBAC equipment, since he had worked on the Coronations for many years. In September its motors were re-fitted to the bogies in the Fitting Shop, and 304 went into the depot compound to be fitted with its trolley, which was filmed. Peter Browne - the electrical engineer - told me that he had heard from retired Frank Hoover that the Coronations had been troublesome. By November 304 was repainted into its original livery by the Paint Shop, and Sheffield 513 was also there, being repainted for the first time since 1985. Kevin did tell me that he had worked with Frank Hoover, who was good at maintaining the Coronations in the depot, while other electricians could not be bothered. Apparently he kept the gap on the rotary-converter correct, along with the silver-tips to make contact, whereas others filed them down. Hence the gap was too great and the contacts did not work, hence the trams did not perform correctly. 304 was under power for the first time on 10th November with Kevin at the controls, and it went up and down track 2 satisfactorily. In December when 304 was in the electrical compound, I heard that there were some problems with the control-wiring. Kevin told me that the wiring to the motors was too short for the bogies to swing-out on curves. Thus, it had now to be rewired again, although it had been driven on a "crawling" notch of the controller, which did not use the VAMBAC equipment. By sheer good fortune Philip Higgs made contact with John Bradley of Toronto, who had been an electrician at the depot and had a set of plans for the equipment, which he would send. He advised that when the Coronation was to be filmed on 6th January, it was to be driven slowly on level track and avoid using the electric braking. On the day, before it left the depot with Philip Higgs at the controls, Jack Nichols - a retired driver and founder of F.T.S. - was filmed giving Philip advice on driving it. Certainly on a sunny day, it was a splendid scene with 304 on the Central Promenade with the Tower, and it was filmed picking up some passengers at Manchester Square, and proceeding to turn on the Pleasure Beach loop. Although more was to follow, Salvage Squad's programme was successful!

(Above) Seen in the depot within a compound, and its separated brake shoes and VAMBAC equipment. (Author)

(Above) Scenes of 304 repanelled in the Body Shop with Balloon 724 and being repainted in its original style. (Author)

(Below) In striking condition at Fleetwood in May 2007. (Author)

(Right) 304 with the Tower and driven by Philip Higgs on its first journey in this Century! (Author)

(Left) 718 being painted in red livery in September 2002. (Right) 643 painted in yellow for advertising. (Author)

During 2002, apart from the restoration of 304, events continued including the derailment of 644 on the Bold Street curve, where it went over the road and demolished the overhead pole. This was caused by the grooved-rail being worn away and therefore the wheels could leave the street-track. Trams were turned round at Ash Street, and the power was turned off in the Ferry area. 754 came on Saturday using its diesel engine, and the crew told me that the new pole would be fitted on Monday. During May trams worked single-line once again between Norbreck and Little Bispham, while tamping was being done to the new ballast. I understand that the relaying work by Birse cost £650,000, one of the first times a firm was commissioned, rather than using their own track-gang, which now had been reduced in size. In June, 724 - the fourth Balloon to be rebuilt like 707 - was seen in the depot mounted on its new under-frame. Stockport 5 was in the compound, with Stan Heaton fitting new upper-deck seats made by Beamish, and Bob Hill was moving the trolley-mounting to the centre of the upper-deck. On Tram Sunday Standard 147 and Stockport 5 travelled down Lord Street with the procession, and reversed on the crossover to return to Ash Street. Here were several more historic trams, including 513, 66, 660 and 40 to operate on the shuttle to Thornton Gate. By this time the track was worn-out and evidenced by the pitching and rolling by the historic trams, especially 4-wheelers like 513. Therefore on 18th October this was confirmed by the Railway Inspector condemning the line from being used by the double-deckers, and thus they were banned and replaced by twin-cars and Centenaries.

(Below) A delightful scene with Stockport 5 in the Tram Sunday procession on 18th July 1999. (Author)

NEW DEVELOPMENTS IN 2003 & 2004

After the filming of 304 on the Promenade in January, Bowyers of Derby were called upon to take the VAMBAC for rebuilding. This was necessary because it had been found that the circular frame had been previously burnt in a fire during service use, also bakelite had been used which had to be replaced. It thus needed re-assembling with a new structure and the internal motor needed rewinding. The cost of this was £6,300, but Salvage Squad gave an extra £5,000 towards the cost, and said that they would feature 304 on another programme. This time the equipment on 304 would include the inverter and batteries as a reserve for the braking, which had not been used since the Sixties. It was interesting that preserved Marton Vambac 11 still had this equipment today. Following the condemnation of the Fleetwood track, work started on its relaying between Thornton Gate and Ash Street, during the winter months. On 12th April 2003, Engineering-car 754 arrived at Fleetwood Ferry, having tested the track, and by 10-00 a.m. the tram service started again, being Easter Saturday 2003. In conversation with Steve Burd, he said that the Balloons would be kept off the Fleetwood route, until this relaying was completed next year. Therefore in 2003 there was a 20-minute service to Fleetwood, using the slow-moving twin-cars and the Centenaries. Tram Sunday would thus include only single-deckers that year, which were 40, 619, 600 & 660, with the Western Train on display at the Ferry, and 633 Trawler "Cevic" at Ash Street. The restoration of the Western Train would cost £100,000, if a sponsor could be found. Unfortunately, 147 was damaged in the depot, when Box 40 had been shunted into it, and so had to be fitted with a new dash panel. Also Sheffield 513 derailed on the reservation, and subsequently as a four-wheeler was banned from travelling north of the Cabin.

I always remember a good show of heritage trams on Sunday 27th July 2003, first seeing Stockport 5 leaving Starr Gate showing HYDE - THROUGH CAR as its destination. As the driver on the open platform passed me, he said "We won't make it". I saw Standard 147 and Boats 604 and 605 between North Pier and Pleasure Beach, whilst on the loop there I saw Bolton 66, Sheffield 513 complete with a monogram on its upper panels, and newly-repainted 602 looking very smart. The duty inspector sent them to a sequence of destinations from Bispham to Tower. Towards the end of August, 304 went out on a trial run at 0530, ready for its filming again by Salvage Squad on 11th September. Being later in the evening they could film it travelling more than 30 m.p.h. past the tableaux and on the new track to Little Bispham.

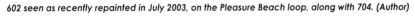

602 seen as recently repainted in July 2003, on the Pleasure Beach loop, along with 704. (Author)

(Above) Sheffield Roberts 513 with coat-of-arms and monogram each in centre of lower and upper panels, with 602 behind.

Also at this time trams were seen in different liveries, including 700 repainted traditionally, and twin-car 673-683 which appeared in yellow and aqua-marine livery of the 11 bus - route. I heard from Engineer Bill Gibson that the relaying of the Fleetwood route would start by the Birse Company in January 2004, completing Broadwater to Rossall Square and Rossall Lane to Westbourne Road. Incidentally the track which was being laid was flat-bottom rail on concrete sleepers, but at the curves double-track was laid in double-chairs, mounted on wooden sleepers. Therefore on 8th November a unique tour was held using the two Coronations 304 & 660, providing the unusual sight of them travelling along the whole of their traditional route. The VAMBAC equipment gave problems on 304, but expert Kevin Graham was able to adjust it en-route, enabling the two Coronations to arrive at the Ferry traditionally.

During this year work started on rebuilding illuminated Frigate 736 in August. Body Shop Manager Mike Airey told me that it would be equipped for permanent service use, and therefore would have a rear side door. Alteration was made to the bows, by reducing their height, and therefore made it clearer for the driver to observe the Promenade. The new saloon roof was more level and therefore supported all the superstructure together with front guns, the bridge and helicopter. An emergency exit was added towards the front of the saloon, these days fulfilling requirements of Health & Safety. When it was completed in September, I quite liked its appearance from the front, but thought that the rear-view was plain, although I had been told it was based on the frigates of Beaver-class. Also the sound of this illuminated tram revealed its origins as Pantograph car 170. The fourth flat-fronted Balloon 724 appeared in a striking bus-route 5 livery of red-and-yellow, as the finale of the style.

(Below) Frigate 736 seen rewiring in the depot compound and at Tram Sunday 17th July 2005, as completed.

(Above) Balloon 713 showing its complete teak-wood frame-work and its metal underframe on blocks.

Because 2004 was the 70th Anniversary of the 26 Balloons, it was intended to have a procession of them, showing a variety of liveries over the years. At the beginning of the year 702 was to be repainted in the Seventies livery thus replacing 708, while 703 in the Eighties livery was fitted with its number 240 over the doors. 712 was repainted in the Sixties livery showing its number 249, and It also had Alhambrinal ceilings and half-drop windows. Unfortunately, in contrast to the others 710 was painted in a bus-style livery of purple-and-yellow, which spoilt the appearance of the tram. However Brush-car 636 was panelled without the roof-windows and was painted in bus-route 14 green-and-yellow livery, which did look quite striking. In the Body-shop Coronation 660 was panelled, and alternate saloon windows were fixed, because some of the winding windows were defective. Since Balloon 713 was being rebuilt, it was to keep its original appearance, being 250 as the first of the second-series. However, during this process it lost its roof windows, fenders and lifeguards, for which they were replaced by a curved-skirt. Mike Airey told me that it had been proposed that one Balloon - 716 or 717 - should be rebuilt with a new under-frame, since B.T.S. had received a donation of £100,000 in the will of Phillip R Thorpe. On Tram Sunday 304 was driven to the Ferry before 0800, for display during the day while 147 and 706 were in procession to open the event. I was told that during the late-October weekend of the Illuminations was the busiest this year, so that 46 trams were in use, although 38 at any one time. At this time I was told that Manchester Square junction was to be relayed by Birse during the winter, and therefore trams were going to use historic Blundell Street and Princess Street track to reach the Promenade.

(Below) 712 in Bold St., Fleetwood having been repainted in post-war livery in June 2004. (Author)

700'S ACCIDENT & TOTALLY TRANSPORT FESTIVAL IN 2005

It was quite interesting to see the trams using the historic Princess Street line once again, when I saw 723 being driven by a learner driver very carefully. I noticed that the junction with the old depot approach line had been welded to avoid derailments here. The Inspector training the drivers said to me; "Why weren't you here this morning at 5 a.m., when the first service-car came this way?" Birse had fenced off the junction at Manchester Square, and by the end of January there was a large pile of rotten wooden sleepers from the track at the north-end. A complete set of new point-work had been delivered by that time, and in conversation with one of the Birse staff he told me that the new track from Germany was encapsulated, which acts as insulation from other piping. In essence, it would prevent the track from becoming corrugated, if totally buried in cement. He said that this job had been given priority by the Railway Inspectors, and the cost would be £900,000. Birse had also quoted for relaying the track to South Pier next winter. The Manchester Square junction would be finished at Easter, but the surface would be completed after. On March 23rd, I was pleased to be there when 643 was brought from the depot and tried the points, and then was driven at speed to Starr Gate, with a cloud of dust being raised from the disused track. Then driver-trainers 711, 722 & 700 arrived at Foxhall, and found they could return to depot via Lytham Road once again. During Easter trams had to use the left-side track only, since the connection had not been made for the north-bound side. However the most dramatic accident happened that weekend on Good Friday, when service-car 700 lost its trolley between Rossall Beach and Westbourne Road stops, which swung round and caught in a bracket-arm, thus removing the trolley from the car. It looked a sad sight, and I believe that the trolley had already de-wired three times on that day, had been reported and received no attention. One Inspector told me that he thought the trolley-head mounting was bent, and thus it was de-wired there by the feeder. I was not surprised when 700 reappeared with a pantograph, which was seen as safer in-service, but did not look as appropriate. Incidentally, on 27th February "By Tram to Foxhall" saw a shuttle-service for 147, 700, 304 & 678 during the day, to give the enthusiasts a chance for an unusual ride. I was also pleased to see Coronation 304 out on testing on 27th April, since it had been fitted with new brake-blocks. I was able to capture it returning to the depot via Princess Street, and subsequently it was seen with 660 for a two-Coronation tour in May.

723 turning into Foxhall Square on 5th July 2005, with the sun providing its profile against a clear sky.

As a driver-training car here, 723 is warning "Beyond the Limits of Fear!". (Author)

At this time the delightful sight of two handsome Coronations contrasted with appearance of Balloons 707 & 709 wholly covered with advertisements. Undoubtedly these were most unsuitable for passengers, since they restricted their viewing especially at night and in the Illuminations. However 715 and 721 looked better, being painted white and carrying MYSTIQUE and HOT ICE for the Pleasure Beach. In June I was sorry that Balloon 711 - the last in the Nineties livery - was repainted to carry an advertisement. Even green-and-cream 702, 703 & 712 had T-shaped advertisements, but Steve Burd gave instructions that 700 & 706 had to purely retain their livery. A new event on the tramway was the Totally Transport Festival on 26th June, organised by L.T.T.. The Promenade was closed from the Starr Inn to Starr Gate, and thus vintage buses were parked along the road facing the sea. Vintage cars were on the other side, and heritage trams operated between North Pier and Starr Gate, including Bolton 66, 147, 304, 660 and four Boats. In the Solaris, models were on display and in the grounds were lots of stalls for transport merchandise. This has become an annual event, making a contrast with the newly-called Transport Festival (Tram Sunday) in Fleetwood. On 10th July V.E. Day to commemorate end of the Second World War was held, 700 and 706 decorated with flags transported the guests from the War Memorial to the Imperial Hotel for lunch, and back in the afternoon to the Central Promenade where there was an air-show. It was very pleasing to see that 700 was again fitted with a trolley, and driven by Graham Twidale wearing the traditional uniform.

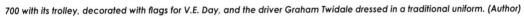

700 with its trolley, decorated with flags for V.E. Day, and the driver Graham Twidale dressed in a traditional uniform. (Author)

SOME RESTORATIONS - INCLUDING MARTON VAMBAC 11

In August, I had a discussion with Chief Engineer Bill Gibson regarding the restoration of the Western Train illuminated tram, and the appeal to Heritage of National Lottery. Apparently they insisted that the tram must be restored as it was created in 1962, then sponsored by ABC TELEVISION illuminated on it. I suggested that the interior of the saloons should be improved on the ghastly shade of pale green on the woodwork. Fortunately this was accepted, since it restored the original interior of former Pantograph 174 as the trailer. Following the necessity to restore the bodies of the Centenary-cars, resulting in new window-frames and panelling, the final 648 went into the Body-shop for such rebuilding. Whereas the others had been changed in their appearance, with higher roof-panels over the windows, larger indicators, and straight windscreens, the N.T.M. insisted that 648 - formerly 651 - maintained its front appearance with curved windscreens and a slim indicator-screen. It happens that it was designated as a preserved-car, and in 2011 it will leave Blackpool for the N.T.M. at Crich. In this month I heard that Brush-car 298 was leaving the Mode Wheel workshop for Crich, where it hopefully would be completed and operated, but not yet! On October 6th, 717 was stripped down to its frame and a new under-frame was built, ready for its restoration, as planned. Unusually, OMO 8 was seen in the Paint-shop, being restored to its original "plum and custard" livery, ready for its departure to the L.T.T. Marton garage. Box 40 followed it into the Paint-shop, where it was rubbed-down and varnished, together with adding the missing lettering "BLACKPOOL & FLEETWOOD" to its front panels. Fortunately it was ready for its annual tour for "Friends of 40", and it was followed into the Paint-shop by 147 to be repainted. Finally in 2005, I heard that Tram Power 611 had arrived from Carnforth, painted in the bus-route 14 livery, but looking better than its plain appearance last time.

Repainted trams towards the end of 2005. (Left) OMO 8 restored in its "plum and custard" livery. (Right) Box 40 having BLACKPOOL & FLEETWOOD restored and was varnished. (Author)

(Above) Like a Marton tram terminus with Vambac 11 and 159 at Carlton Colville, East Anglia. (Bryan Grint)

Undoubtedly the greatest event in the tramway museums was the restoration and launching of Marton Vambac 11 at the East Anglia Transport Museum, Carlton Colville on Easter Saturday 26th March 2005. Originally it was saved from Marton Depot by being hired for a tour in January 1963 by Keith Terry. Thus it joined Dreadnought 59 for a last run along the Promenade to Starr Gate, and was then stored in Bispham Depot while its fellow-cars were broken-up. It then went to Hayling Island for a proposed light-rail system there, and when this did not happen East Anglia Museum acquired it. 11 operated between 1978 and 1984, looking much like it did on the Marton route, and then it was withdrawn prior to complete restoration. While work was done on the body there, the VAMBAC equipment went to Den Haag for attention, but had to be recovered and sent to Bowyers of Derby, to be reconstructed, as that of 304. I first saw 11 in September, waiting at the terminus with Standard 159 and Manchester trolleybus 1344, built by Burlinghams. Certainly 11 looked as it did when first introduced to the Marton route in 1948, with the flares in the livery, chrome windscreens, and the cream housing for the VAMBAC equipment. In the saloon I saw it had newly-upholstered seats, fluorescent lighting, half-drop windows and glass-screens for the platform, all looking very cheerful. Riding on it and hearing the clicking of the equipment, provided the quick acceleration which gave it success in Blackpool. It was also delightful to ride and drive Standard 159, and see London HR2 1878 and Amsterdam 474 together with Lowestoft 14 being rebuilt in the Works. Of course it is hoped that Vambac 11 will be seen in Blackpool for the 125th Anniversary celebrations in 2010, in exchange for a Boat car.

With its original destination, 11 leaves London 1858 as the next tram. (Bryan Grint)

2006 - 2007 GOOD NEWS ABOUT 717 & BAD NEWS OF 611

The interesting aspects of 2006 was the presence of 717 in the Fitting Shop for new air-pipes, and I was told that it would have the traditional pointed-front, with new curved windows at two levels and twin indicators. Certainly it happened that original features were incorporated in the rebuilding, including the arch in the centre of the roof and half-drop windows in the saloons, together with Alhambrinal ceilings. To achieve this, it was necessary to remove such parts from withdrawn Balloons 704 and 716. Out on the tramway the sight of articulated Tram Power 611 indicated it accumulated hours of satisfactory operation, as demanded by the Railway inspector, before it was allowed to carry people. I therefore went to meet Professor Lewis Lesley at the depot, to find out something about the nature of its situation. He first told me that 611 had been stored in Cardiff, and was then moved to Carnforth where it was fitted with new more-compact motors and alternators under the front-floor. The weight of 611 was 22 tonnes, had a folding-ramp for wheelchairs, and the driver had a foot-pedal to operate track-brakes. Unfortunately 611's centre-section wheels had a derailment on Starr Gate loop, but Lewis Lesley claimed that the grooved-rail was worn and thus the wheels climbed-out. On Tram Sunday 611 was on display at Fleetwood Ferry, and open to the public who completed 400 questionnaires with their opinion. Certainly it was good to see on its return to Blackpool over the sleeper-track, through the fields at Rossall. However, its finale came on 24th January 2007, when its driver Alan Williams could smell a burning under the floor, left the car at Manchester Square to pull-down the pantograph, by which time it was full of smoke and flames, which destroyed half of the tram. Of course Lewis Lesley on television that night said that it never had any problems until now! From the statement given by Steve Burd, it indicated that this would be investigated, and in reality its chance of carrying passengers at Blackpool was finished.

(Left) 717 with wooden framework on top deck and metal framework for the cab.
(Right) 611 and 304 on Tram Sunday 2006. (Below) Final view of 611 at Cleveleys on 17th January 2007, before its fire. (Author)

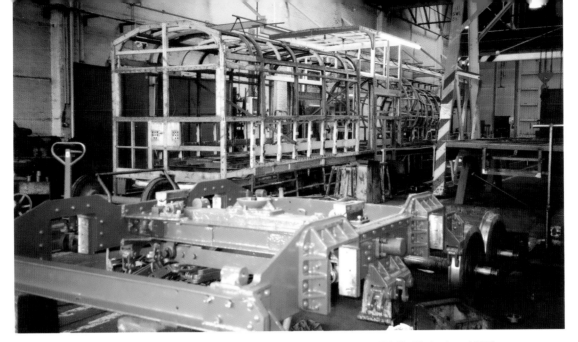

In the foreground bogies, and wooden frame of 733-734 Western Train from railcoach 209 in the Works, August 2007.

On October 4th 2006 came the good news that Heritage Lottery Fund would donate a grant of £278,000 to restore the Western Train to its original condition. This facilitated the building of a new under-frame for the locomotive 733, for which towing-car 677 would be used. Regarding the trailer 734, some research into the appearance of its original saloon was inspired by Pantograph 167 at Crich. While the Western Train had always been popular with the public, the famous Cliff Richard said: "It would be sad to imagine Blackpool without its historic trams. I have fond recollections of my trip on this famous tram in 1963." Of course it launched the opening of a new ABC Theatre on 31st March 1963, with "Holiday Carnival" starring Cliff Richard & the Shadows. In August 2006 Blackpool Tramway was allocated emergency funding of £11.8 million for relaying track between Manchester Square and Waterloo Road, together with Fleetwood Copse Road sub-station. Steve Burd said: "The funding arrived in the nick of time, since the track had been deteriorating, and the speed of the trams has reduced to 4 m.p.h.". During the winter Birse undertook this job, while between Beach Road and Thornton Gate the track was relayed by Blackpool track-gang. While buses operated the route from Starr Gate to Thornton Gate, trams operated to Fleetwood, using five Centenary cars. Talking to the track-gang foreman, he told me that new track was ordered and delivered to the site, without them having to move it by themselves as previously. Flat-bottom rail is now being used - as originally by the Tramroad Company - and on concrete-sleepers with spring-clips. He thought that next winter they would probably relay Little Bispham loop, which happened.

The new frame of Western Train using the saloon of 677 and wood-frame strengthened by metal framework, in the Body-Shop. (Author)

In 2007 the 70th anniversary of Brush-cars, was commemorated by repainting 623 in the wartime livery, seen here at Cleveleys and Pleasure Beach. (Author)

In 2007 the development of the service-trams in the fleet was more relevant with 720 - the last with 84 seats - was stripped-down, ready for building a new under-frame. It was then planned to be fitted with new doors operated by the driver, and its platform to be widened to meet the boarding-platforms. 717 was in the electrical compound being re-wired and fitted with the 24-volt A/C alternator, fitted under the stairs. Looking at this tram again, it was clear that the original teak frame was still robust, but the ends had been rebuilt in a metal-frame. Since 2007 was the 70th Anniversary of the Brush-cars, 623 was repainted in the wartime green-and-cream livery, to distinguish it from the others covered with advertising. During the winter of 2007-8 Little Bispham loop was relayed in grooved rail, together with new point-work from Austria. Down at the Pleasure Beach a new loop-line was being constructed by Birse, with a one-way layout to change its original design. In North Shore, another firm Colas relayed all the track from Gynn Square to Norbreck, with 3-track layout at Bispham and a simple crossover at the Cabin, without the loop. In March, at Fleetwood a new sub-station was being built at Copse Road, replacing the original one in the old depot building, and followed by one at Broadwater. On 20th July 2008, the newly-restored Balloon 717 in its Thirties livery appeared and operated a shuttle between Fisherman's Walk and North Pier for Tram Sunday. A week later I organised a tour on 717, giving us a chance to enjoy recapturing the feel of a vintage ride, and photographing it with 700 and 703, representing Balloons in different generations.

(Below) The first tour on restored 717 was 26th July 2008 showing it in the original style of livery and trolley. Subsequently it lost its trolley, and was fitted with a pantograph, as seen on the Ferry curve. (Author)

A delightful view of the Western Train arriving at Fleetwood Ferry on 14th May 2009, looking as it did originally in 1963! (R.P.Fergusson)

ABOUT TO EXCHANGE THE PAST WITH THE FUTURE

in March 2008 came the news that £85.3 million pounds was awarded to Blackpool for upgrading the tramway, now 123 years old. While £60.3 came from the Government, Blackpool Borough and Lancashire County Council has to contribute £12.5 million each. Bearing in mind that the tramway was reaching its 125th Anniversary in 2010, having made constant effort to modernise the fleet over many years, it now seemed that it should become a modern light-rail system. As Steve Burd said: "This investment from the Government will guarantee the long-term future of the tramway". Therefore it was now possible to buy new trams, in the form of five-section articulated cars with low-floors to improve boarding facilities for the passengers, including the disabled. The newly funded scheme included the relaying of track over the whole system, including street track in Fleetwood. All tram stops are to be provided with platforms level with the trams, and the number of stops will be reduced from 62 to 37, at a greater distance of 475 metres apart. Thus the full journey-time over the system will be 55 minutes. This will also be facilitated by the road crossings to be controlled by the trams, and giving them priority over the road traffic. Finally, a new depot and works was to be originally constructed in Blundell Street, but this was changed to Starr Gate, despite the objection of the residents. Construction started in 2009, in the form of a 40-foot high building on the site of the car-park and turning-circle there. Since the 16 articulated cars, being built by Bombardier in Vienna, cost 2 million pounds each and need a more modern and secure depot, at a cost of £20 million pounds. The new fleet will begin to arrive in 2011, and the old fleet will begin to depart for tramway museums, leaving roughly 24 of the historic cars left here. This will include ten rebuilt Balloons, three Boats, four illuminated cars and six heritage cars representing the fleet's history. In 2010 and 2011 the trams will not operate during the winter, owing to the final relaying of Promenade sections of track. During the Season of 2010, the 125th Anniversary will be celebrated by the presence of historic trams from five Tramway Museums. This will represent the contrast of the past with the future era commencing in 2012. It is therefore hoped that the future of the Blackpool Tramway will be as successful as it has been since 1885, for 125 years!

A CHALLENGE FOR THE FUTURE

by Trevor Roberts, Managing Director , Blackpool Transport Services

In 2009 a joint project by the Department of Transport, Lancashire County Council and Blackpool Council was announced to invest over £100 million to totally upgrade the Tramway. The tram line is considered a key transport asset on the Fylde Coast, and it has been considered essential that the Tramway is upgraded to ensure firstly that the service continues to operate for future generations, secondly to encourage and enhance re-generation and inward investment in the Fylde, and thirdly to bring the service straight into the twenty-first Century.

The key features include 16 new Bombardier articulated-trams featuring low-floors, accessible for all users, including passengers with disabilities. Each tram costs in excess of £2 million pounds, and will be operated by state-of-the-art driver controls. There will be new location tram stops featuring level access, which means that they will be compliant with the Disability Discrimination Act, and eight kilometres of track will be renewed. Along the line there will be 14 priority signals installed at highway junctions to improve journey-times, and a large new depot and servicing-facility is being built at Starr Gate.

The investment of £68.3 million pounds comes from the Department of Transport, £17.7 million from Blackpool Council, 15.2 from Lancashire County Council and £0.4 million from INTEREG. North West Europe programme will build on the current regeneration projects taking place in the town, whilst further improving access to the Fylde Coast. The stated aim of the upgrades are to provide a high quality transport facility along the Fylde Coast, appropriate for the twenty-first century, in order to provide quicker journey times for passengers, provide level boarding for all passengers - including using wheelchairs, carrying heavy shopping and the less-mobile disabled - thus to encourage the use of public transport along the whole of the Fylde Coast.

Whilst the investment is most welcome, and ensures that the Tramway will continue for the future, the past is not being forgotten. Of the present fleet, there will be ten modified Balloon trams which will complement the overall service by the new trams, and are currently being rebuilt with automatic doors and better entrances, to facilitate passengers boarding and alighting. Additionally, the Company are retaining six heritage trams and three illuminated trams which will be used as tourist and heritage attractions. The operation of old and new together is going to be an interesting challenge, and one that will need careful co-ordination so that the heritage trams do not delay the modern operation of the service.

It is a challenge and opportunity which Blackpool Transport staff look forward to meeting with enthusiasm, when the whole upgrade comes on-line in April 2012.